SAL ~~~AN
WITH AN
AK
47

Best Regards.

Alan Barry

THE CLOISTER HOUSE PRESS

First published in 2015
This edition published in 2016 by
The Cloister House Press

ISBN 978-1-909465-54-1

Dedications

MY FATHER WILLIAM JOSEPH BARRY 1936 - 2009

"When I was a boy of 14, my father was so ignorant I could hardly stand to have the old man around. But when I got to be 21, I was astonished at how much the old man had learned in seven years."

Mark Twain

NIGEL STUART CLARIDGE – 1966-2006

A fine Grenadier, Father, Son, Brother and Friend

Stand down Guardsman, your duty is done. May you rest in peace.

ACKNOWLEDGEMENTS

Thank you to my wonderful children, Nathan, Catherine and Connor for making me a very proud and lucky father. Without your love and support the world would be a lesser place.

Thank you to Violet, for giving me the greatest gift I have received, our three wonderful children.

Thank you to my wonderful Mother Ethna. I could not have wished for more love and caring throughout my life.

To my brother Colin and my sister Yvonne for their support and love throughout my life.

My best friend Mark Weir for dragging me back from the abyss in 2010.

Thomas Bartlett for his help and advice in writing this book, I could have never achieved this without him.

Last but not least, thanks to my loyal friend Paul Stokes whose support and assistance on this project has been invaluable.

Contents

I HAVE NEVER FORGOTTEN THE
THINGS THAT SAVED MY LIFE

May 2006 Kabul, Afghanistan

The dirt kicked up high as the Hummer sped through – aliens on an Afghan moon. The wrong people, in the wrong land, at the wrong time. The story of my life. But then it was not my life: I was sitting a couple of miles up the road in my office inside our secure building in Kabul.

The Hummer collided with the taxi, panicked, drove over the occupants and fired a 50cal machine gun into the crowd killing between 2 and 12 people, depending on who you asked. There were a lot of viewpoints, and even more blame. The crowd began to buck and seethe. Writhing in the Kabul trap, caught between the Taliban, the Americans, the Afghan Army and Police, poverty, history and the surrounding mountains; ancient pressures pushing and re-forming them. I was sitting at my desk oblivious when the crowd turned violent. So many reasons: the bodies on the ground; the bodies in front of them; and the Hummer, a beacon of America and a natural target for Afghan aggression.

The Afghan mob, crowd, or insurgents had decided they were going to storm Afghan Wireless's office building. I was inside minding my own business, rolling out the telecommunications network and working on benign sales targets, team building and staff training. The word came in, the crowd, the mob, the locals were gathered outside. There was an AK47 propped against the wall beside me, beside me is where I kept it. I also had a Glock side arm on my hip, or maybe it was in my drawer as I was in the office. A long time ago I'd learned the hard way not to sit around with a loaded weapon.

The three thousand strong mob were intent on storming the compound in righteous anger, directed at us and every other building that screamed establishment at them. I'd made the decision that I would not be taken alive a long time ago in a different place. This was not my first mob, nor my first riot. Old training kicked in, before the sales training and telecommunications, back into the mists of things I don't talk about. But I have never forgotten the things that have saved my life.

Looking out across the ancient bullet ridden skyline, I thought to myself that I could probably make it across the roof tops outside, at least I wouldn't be penned in and I'd have the chance to escape. The mountains looked on watching everything, unmoved.

Thankfully the doors and gates to our building held. Everything outside the compound, every vehicle or sign was destroyed, the security hut burnt to a cinder. I knew how the mob felt. Afghanistan; that's how they felt.

Afghanistan

Afghanistan, more than anywhere else I've ever been on earth exists in a perpetual state of flux – destruction and creation, the mountains, the crumbling walls, fragile allegiances – construction to destruction. The mountains, the representation of the earth's fissures and man's conflicts.

I had been holding it together a little bit myself of late. Was this the inciting moment? Yeah, that and twenty years of success and failure, maybe throw in some Northern Ireland, some love and loathing. All the little pieces that went together to make me. Pieces now falling away as I found myself once more in the breach. Pretty much where I liked to be. I never would have said I enjoyed the danger, but looking back I have always courted it. Often ran straight towards it.

The mob moved on and destroyed an aid organisation and some more ISAF[1] platitudes about improving security and moving forward. The Taliban were back; making every alarm, every incident more heightened. I went back to my desk, sat down and tried to remember where I was and what the hell I was doing there.

---

1 ISAF International Security Assistance Force. Nato led security force in Afghanistan.

Chapter 2
LOSING OUR INNOCENCE

1964 Dublin

I was born in Holles Street Hospital, Dublin, without a problem in the world. My Dad was a fitter, repairing machinery in Bachelors, my Mother a house wife, both from Cabra. Both intent on getting out of Dublin as soon as possible to rear their family. I'm the eldest of three. It wasn't much longer before we rocked up on the concrete shores of Birmingham in 1966 and Dad secured a job in Cadbury Schweppes, trebling his salary. My parents were trying to move up, like most immigrants they wanted to change their lives and those of their children. That is the way it went in those days in Ireland, stay poor or leave.

I've vague memories of our first stop in Birmingham, Slade Road, Erdington, near the site of today's spaghetti junction. It was much like living in any working class community in Dublin. After a year my parents sent me back to Ireland to live with my grandmother. As a child it didn't make much difference to me. I was used to it before I knew not to be. I lived with my grandparents for a year and every couple of months either my Nan would take me over to visit my parents or they would come back to Dublin for a few days. My parents where Irish immigrants and like many before chose to work as many hours as they could in order to save up enough money to purchase a house in a more upmarket area. My parents achieved this in a nice residential area of Birmingham called Sutton Coldfield. We were on the up. England had allowed us to change our lives.

My parents were practicing, but not strict Catholics. We would go to mass some Sundays but not all. Our primary school was a different matter: St Peter and St Paul's. It was so Catholic it could have been in Ireland. The only thing they taught you there was how to pray, how to pray and how to take a beating. The headmaster Mr Minister was a sadist. It was a brutal regime. Everyday some boy would get a hiding, and I mean a clobbering. I was no different and regularly found myself on the wrong end of the headmasters' fists or his hand. In the wrong place at the wrong time, perhaps it was the beginning of a theme? Mr Minister was a strict Catholic. Whatever about that, he used to commit acts of savagery on children I've seldom seen since.

Mr Minister never caned us; he punched us, punched the living daylights out of us. We boys had to wear short trousers all year round, so we'd feel the sting of his slaps on our legs until we got older and graduated to his punching. He picked on all the boys, never the girls. Once during communion, I failed to find the way back to my pew quickly enough. In between the punches he memorably told me I'd been "chewing the host like chewing gum". After another infringement, when I'd apparently been using my fork incorrectly, he pushed my face into my dinner and held it there.

I remember when I first started in St Peter and St Paul's, I did get bullied by this one boy, Martin Pitt. Mum still recalls the story and tells it admitting she was terrified herself. I was walking home one day, my mum saw me getting hassled and she came over and asked me:

"Why are you letting him pick on you like that? Look at you, you get two strong meals a day."

It felt like a mixture of permission and instruction. So he did it again and I gave him what he was looking for, the six year old version anyway. And that was the end of that. I was never a bully. I didn't like bullies and even to this day I don't like them. I never went looking for trouble, but if someone came looking for it, I certainly wouldn't have walked away. From then on my mum never worried about me, she knew I could take care of myself.

I was very lucky with my mum. In many ways she was the best mum a man could ever want. She was very loving, generous, always there for us. My Dad was like a lot of Irish men in those days: often taciturn and somewhat withdrawn. There were two sides to him, the good Billy and the bad Billy, and when he'd had a drink the bad Billy would come out.

We weren't very well disciplined as children. None of us were. My parents worked full time, so my brother, my sister and I were brought up by my grandmother. Your granny, as most can attest to, will always cut you a little bit more slack. When my Nan died years later, I was completely devastated. It was like losing a parent we were so close. I was twenty eight when she died. She was a wonderfully wise woman and a Scorpio, so she was a handful.

My parents worked hard to ensure we grew up in a pleasant suburb of Birmingham. We lived directly opposite Pype Hayes Park. It functioned as our whole world in those days. We'd disappear in the morning, spend the day in the park, make a den in a tree, or build a raft with a pallet and float on it across the lake. Carefree days, like Brummie Huckleberry Finns. Some of the things I got up to I'd be horrified to hear my own children had been doing the same, but all us parents grow up to be a little hypocritical.

At the age of fourteen I started coming to Ireland every summer. My cousin John lived in Artane in Dublin. The two of us were great mates. I simply became a member of John's family while I was staying with them. Mostly John and I listened to heavy metal and went to the famous Grove disco in Clontarf. I've remained close with my father's sister Bridie and her husband Sean since and they are still a part of my life today. A truly wonderful couple and a great advertisement for marriage.

Whenever I was back in Ireland I'd also spend time with my uncle Mark who owned a plant hire shop. Mark served as a role model of sorts for me as a teenage lad. A great all round guy and truly fantastic salesman. Even in Ireland, the home of great talkers, he was considered a brilliant salesman. I'd like to think I learned a thing or two about sales working with him. Those summers, while most adults were still treating me as a child, Mark would bring me out boozing to nightclubs and set me up with girls. Naturally I slightly idolised him.

Bishop Walsh Catholic, my Secondary School in Sutton Coldfield, was a lovely place, situated in a beautiful part of the city, alongside fabulous fields and generally a really green natural environment. I continued my Boy's Own childhood there, excelling in sport. I was quite bright but I never really applied myself to learning or study. I could run the 100 metres in 11.4 seconds at the age of fifteen. As a member of Lozells Harriers Athletic Club, I competed regularly at athletics events. Our parents had made it clear they wanted us to get a job after we left school so grades were never that important. As kids, despite the fact we were left to our own devices, we were always aware of a loving safety net around us.

I've had a lifelong interest in the military and I was a member of the air force cadets in school and the scouts. I grew up loving war movies and adventure, spending any free time off with mates having war games in the woods, Swallows and Amazons, well our version anyway.

I suppose I was born a bit reckless. Summer 1973 booting along on my Chopper bicycle a good friend of mine on the back, we had a desperate accident. I fractured my femur. I'll always remember me sobbing, my Dad
carrying me to his car, a Hillman Imp, driving to the hospital. I was in agony. Very few injuries feel like a broken femur in the back of a Hillman Imp. The phenomenal number of bumps shuddered the pain and agony through my bones right into my soul – or so the ten year old me thought.

In the Birmingham Accident Hospital they put me in traction for two months. Being only ten, when I heard the loud explosion I didn't really understand what it was. I didn't hear the second one, or maybe I only heard the second one, they were only ten minutes apart. I'll remember the night of sirens forever though. Later the bombs became known as the Birmingham Pub Bombings. 21 predominantly young people died in those two explosions, with 182 people injured. For Birmingham it was one of the worst nights in its history. The city felt betrayed by the Irish community and grieved for their young dead.

Savagery

Doctor Henry Proctor had operated on my femur. In the days and hours after the bombings, he operated on many of those brought in. Dr Proctor was also interviewed on the television after the bombings particularly on the extent of the injuries. Unforgettably the wood from the pubs' furniture made the surgeons' jobs infinitely more difficult because wood was not detectable by X-ray. This small grim detail still makes me shudder with its lethal implications.

Doctor Proctor spoke about the horror on TV news and what he said has echoed through the city ever since; everyone in Birmingham remembers their own awful souvenir alongside the deaths. For me I'll remember forever him talking about:

"one man with a chair leg right up his thigh, entering at the knee and going right up to the groin."

Birmingham Accident Hospital was a world leading major injuries unit at the time but they couldn't save everyone. No one could.

It was a horrifying ordeal for Birmingham. The British, and the people of Birmingham were understandably angry. We can say what we like about the British, but they normally didn't hold the IRA against us. The bombings in Birmingham were different. My Dad, a real Paddy, and universally liked, was told to stay home from work. My sister was kept home from school because it was known as an Irish Catholic school. There was so much animosity towards the Irish in the city. The windows in the Irish Centre were smashed in and many people were almost ashamed to be Irish or associated with Ireland for a period after the bombings.

But the British and the locals in Birmingham let us go back to our daily lives. My sister and I returned to school, my Dad to work.

There were two other bombings that the British took very personally: Warrington, when the IRA killed a child on the high street; Guildford, when they targeted a couple of soldier's bars, I used to drink in them myself in the years after. But to plant two bombs in Birmingham, in two bars frequented solely by young people, there was no justification for that. Shooting a soldier in Northern Ireland, we were considered a legitimate target, I could get my head around that, but the Birmingham Pub Bombings scarred a city for life. It robbed children of their futures and parents of their lives' sanity.

The IRA lost their way killing innocent civilians. They blew away their supposed legitimacy. A legitimate target is a person you consider the enemy, not just because they are a national of that country. You certainly don't kill women and children. The old IRA never did that. They killed G-men, British soldiers, Irish Constabulary, spies, whatever. They didn't go around killing women and kids.

The Birmingham Pub Bombings are something I remember from my childhood, but they did not have any profound influence on me at the time because of the simple fact that I was too young.

Years later I met Lord Chief Justice Denning at a drinks reception in London whilst I was a serving Guardsman at the Palace. I'd been invited to the evening by my then girlfriend, who lived in Lincoln's Inn Fields in the apartment below Lord Denning. I got chatting to him, and when he found out I was a serving soldier from Birmingham, he was not afraid to speak openly. What he didn't know was that my parents were both Irish Catholics. How would he?

The first thing he mentioned was the Birmingham Six. The campaign to have them released meant they were very much in the news at the time. Lord Denning simply stated that in his opinion, despite the Birmingham Six being guilty, due to overzealous police work the case was going to collapse. He talked about how if Britain had capital punishment we would not have these problems, as the Six would be dead. A not uncommon view at the time particularly in the midst of the British Establishment.

Denning, along with many others at the time, was convinced the Six were guilty. The investigation in to the Birmingham Pub Bombings was an incompetent police operation, marred by brutality and witness coercion. The police botched it and wasted lives and time convicting six innocent people rather than finding the true culprits. Lord Denning famously remarked when asked whether the Six should be allowed to appeal, that the repercussions for the English legal establishment if they were found innocent would be worse than six innocent people serving life in prison.

"This is such an appalling vista that every sensible person in the land would say that it cannot be right that these actions should go any further."

When I was growing up I considered myself British, despite my parents being Irish. I went to school in England, I had a British education, learnt British history. I was British as far as I was concerned. It wasn't until I served in Northern Ireland that I started to wonder.

Chapter 3
THE ELITE OF THE BRITISH ARMY

79 Battle honours.
I left school in 1982, just after Maggie got in. Unemployment was rife, and the waiting list for the RAF was over a year. Instead I applied for the RAF regiment – the soldiers that guard the airfields. There was a recession and Maggie was sorting out the mess. Other than the army, the infamous Youth Training Scheme was the only thing you could do around that time. Most employers used the YTS as an excuse for free labour. Infuriatingly, even after I passed the RAF entrance exam, I was still looking at a six month waiting list. I was getting fed up tapping my foot and kicking my heels with part time work; I was anxious for some action.

Walking home past the Army Careers Office one fateful day, something inside caught my eye, a picture of the trooping of the colour and all those magnificent red tunics and bear skins outside Buckingham Palace. I walked in as seriously as I could, and spoke to the recruiter,

"I'd like to join the Irish Guards."

He looked me up and down before replying,

"The Guards no way, you're not tall enough lad. Actually hold on. Maybe you would just about scrape in. Come over here and I'll measure you."

Five foot eight and a half was the regulation, and luckily:

"Five foot eight and a half, you just scraped it. Come back tomorrow and do the entrance exam."

I passed and within two weeks I was at recruit selection in front of an officer. The officer gave me some great advice:

"You scored 85% in the entrance exam, you shouldn't be going into the Guards or any infantry regiment. You should get a trade, join the Royal Electrical Mechanical Engineers, or the Air Corps."

But I was not to be dissuaded by good advice. I was adamant.

"I want to be a Guardsman",

"Why do you want to be a Guardsman?" looking right into my eyes.

"I don't know, I just do."

"It's not the uniform is it?" he asked peering right into my mind.

"No, no it's not. It's because they are the elite of the British Army." I said dead earnest sticking my chest out.

I was telling the truth, that's really what it was, well that and the uniform. I admit it, when I looked at that uniform I was star struck. All I could think about was how dignified I'd look. But much more than that I'd always wanted to be the best, to be top of the tree. It's been the same my whole life. And for me the Guards were the best, the elite of the British Army and they still are today.

My great grandfather had been a Scots Guard. I had no affinity for the Scots Guards as I was not Scottish, but I'd been hearing about the Guards all my life. The Irish Guards were not looking for recruits that day and the Grenadiers had two battalions to maintain, so I ended up joining the Grenadiers. The Grenadiers are known as the First Regiment of Foot Guards, because they are the only regiment to have stayed loyal to the British Crown throughout their history. The Grenadiers are the most senior regiment of infantry in the British Army. They wanted the best and trained us to be the best.

After King Charles was executed, the Grenadiers were formed as a Royalist regiment in exile in 1656. Due to problems after the death of Cromwell, the British decided they did actually want a monarchy and Charles's son Charles II came back in 1660. Grenadiers are called the First Regiment of Foot as part of the Household Division. When I saw the bear skins the Grenadiers wore, I knew that was what I wanted. After the regiment had defeated Napoleon at the Battle of Waterloo, they were given the bear skin as a battle honour as well as their name. It was the headdress of the French Imperial Guards. I wanted some of that.

My mum saw me to the train at New Street Station in Birmingham the day I left for basic training. She cried, I am pretty sure it was the first time I'd ever seen my mother cry. On the train from Waterloo to Brookwood Surrey it was obvious who was going down to Guards' training. We'd been instructed to wear a suit when we left the barracks, this included the journey down and each of us looked as gawky and awkward as the other. I looked around and thought to myself, I won't be hanging around with some of these lads. I didn't like the look of half of them.

As soon as we disembarked we were met by a six feet tall sergeant shouting and roaring at us to get on the buses. One recruit took one look, turned right around and got straight back on the train. We were brought to Pirbright, the Guards' Depot. There were five regiments of foot: Grenadier, Scots, Irish, Welsh and Coldstream Guards and two regiments of Cavalry; Blues and Royals, and the Lifeguards. We were all trained together. Everyone's training was six months long and pretty much identical.

I joined up at the height of the miners' strike. A lot of the recruits had been miners. Many of them had worked in the Derbyshire and Macclesfield Collieries. Unsurprisingly, one skill all the ex-miners possessed was the ability to dig trenches like demons, which in the infantry comes in really handy. The Northerners seemed to be from a different planet. Their planet liked gravy on their chips instead of salt and vinegar and seemed to speak a different language. I hadn't a clue what they were saying half the time. There were a lot of working class accents, 80% of Number 10 platoon was made up of boys from Manchester. The army wasted no time in training us in drill and regimentation, how to be Guardsmen.

The first day most recruits could not march, so we were walked down to the barbers, then given all the kit we'd need as soldiers, except our rifles, which were kept in the armoury. The first day slid by in a blur of administration. The regimentation was already afoot.

For the next six months there was a sergeant standing around screaming at us at all times.

"Mark time. Left right left right." The marching and the shouting was endless.

Lance Sergeant Wilson was a Coldstream Guard and Platoon Sergeant Morgan was a Welsh Guard. They trained us. Together they had a warped sense of humour, often making us laugh even when we were in pain – both great army characters. I remember all of us outside for sports day exhaling plumes of steamy air when Sergeant Morgan bounded up and asked who fancied playing football, rugby and so on. Before we started to peel off to our chosen sport, Sergeant Morgan added generously,

"I have a special on today. Darts? Anybody, game of darts?" What could be better?

The two unfittest guys in the platoon put their hands up, with visions of themselves throwing darts down the Naffi[2]. With a glint in his eye, Sergeant Morgan looked at them and said,

"Great. You two can go for a dart round the cross country course."

We all laughed as the two wheezed their way around the course. Any chance to laugh was taken. That's army humour for you, always slightly functional. We attended classes all day, learning about combat, weapons' instruction, drill instruction, fitness, first aid, and so on. Every platoon was broken down into four man sections called bricks, the same as when we joined our battalion. In the evenings as we polished our boots the NCOs quizzed us on regimental history, ensuring we understood we were to be part of a long line of Guardsmen, and how important the Grenadier's history was.

We were recruits until we passed out. I never met any other Irish while I was there. The army knew about my Irish birth. Not sure if anyone else knew. If they did they never mentioned it. If you'd asked me I would have said I was British. I didn't accept that I was Irish at the time.

Army training in those days was all about breaking you – much more so than it is now apparently. However, it was not the nightmare often portrayed in the movies, well not for me

2 Navy Army Airforce a type of social club were we used to play darts.

anyway. Yeah, we were beaten physically if we fell on the ground, and if the Non Com Officers (NCOs) thought we were faking it, they would kick us until we stood back up. When one recruit was perceived to have a hygiene problem, we were told to give him a bath. Some of the other recruits put him in a bath with Vim, the scouring agent, and all his equipment. The screams were awful. I balked at this type of thing. I just thought it was cruel. The NCOs used the recruits whom they knew would comply. The Guards did not suffer fools gladly; they wanted tough soldiers that would not break.

The Commandant's 'March and Shoot' half way through training was seen as an ideal way to get rid of weak recruits. We had to run ten miles in full kit; thirty six pounds of equipment, our rifle, our helmet, all as a squad. Next we had to do an assault course. At the end of the assault course we had to carry another recruit in all his kit in a fireman's lift for one hundred metres. Finally, we had marksmanship on the live firing range where we had to score at least 75%. If we failed at any stage, we would be back-squaded. Back-squaded meant being taken out of the platoon and sent back, normally a month, which meant doing the 'March and Shoot' all over again.

The overarching feeling during basic training was anxiety: anxiety that we'd get back squaded or worse, fail training altogether. This was my memory of it anyway. Many failed. I think out of seventy four of us in number 10-11 platoon, only twenty six made it through. I really wanted to be a Guardsman.

Sometimes we'd be given passes to the local town, Guildford. Saturday night was squaddie night out. We'd march hopefully down to the Guard Room in our shirt and tie, stand to attention. The Sergeant would inspect us, anyone not deemed smart enough was not allowed out. Guildford is down the road from Aldershot, hence the paratroopers would be out as well wearing their normal civilian dress; desert boots, jeans and a bomber jacket. There is massive rivalry and competition amongst all regiments but especially between the Guards Division and the Parachute Regiment; both consider themselves the best. The discipline insured there were never any fights. All of us were hammering the pints down, but we were mega fit, we could just throw it off us. Drinking ten pints was no problem, we'd swim home and be up fast and strong the next day.

Sandhill was a hill made of sand designed to sap every ounce of energy out of you by the time you reached the top, echoes of the Sean Connery movie *The Hill* from 1965. It was so gruelling that it was often used as a punishment alongside the regular climbs that were an integral part of our training. My own squad had to do it once in our number one dress when we were adjudged to be insufficiently turned out for one of the Adjutant's inspections. Our Platoon Sergeant marched us to Sandhill and beasted us up and down it again and again. That in itself was awful, but worse was trying to get our number one dress clean for a week afterwards. The Four Sisters was another famous Guards' training landmark: four hills that we all got to know very well over the six months as we climbed up and down them day and night in full kit; all 36 pounds of it.

The Bayonet Assault Course remains one of the most singular experiences of my life, never mind something difficult that stands out from the Guards' training. We all knew it was coming, the day began with a good old fashioned beasting , a three mile run in full kit, stopping for press ups and sit ups. A couple of trips up Sandhill. Pushing us to our limits, and winding us up and up as tight as they could. This was nothing new, but that day there was an extra edge to everything, that day we knew we were going to do the Bayonet Assault Course.

Every infantry soldiers needs to know how to use a bayonet.

The assault course consisted of pits of mud to wade through, burning tyres to jump over, thunder flash grenades, real grenades without shrapnel being lobbed at us, GPMGs[3] being fired over our heads with blank rounds: basically mayhem. The army wanted to replicate a battle, to induce the near psychosis needed to mount a bayonet assault at an armed enemy.

Amidst the chaos at the starting line, a lone Scots Guard stood playing 'The Crags of Tumbledown Mountain' on his bag

3 General Purpose Machine Gun

pipes. The tune was composed in the Falklands War by a Scots Guard in the aftermath of the battle. It is a tribute to the Scots Guards' heroic bayonet assault on the summit of Tumbledown Mountain. With ammunition running low, the command was given to fix bayonets. The first person into the enemy position was Major Kiszely, who was awarded a military cross for his bravery. The charge was one of the last bayonet charges by the British Army.

We lined up individually to attempt the course, each with our blood boiling over. We all knew what the bag pipes signified and together with the sounds of war coming from the assault course and our previous three hours exertions we were amped up higher than we'd ever been.

"Fix bayonets" the NCO roared at us, a command that sends ferocious shivers juddering up the spine of every British soldier.

This was followed by the NCO shouting brutal descriptions of what the enemy had done to our families.

"They killed your family.
They raped your sister and your mother,
Then they murdered all of them."
Louder and louder. Screaming at us by this stage.
"What is a bayonet for?" they yelled.
And we screamed in answer, each like a raging animal,
"To kill."
"What are you going to do with it?"
"Kill."

We roared our raging reply fully believing it. We went screaming as we tore along. One by one we charged, sprinting, going full pace over each obstacle, only pausing to plunge our bayonets into the uniformed enemy dummies. The training and the adrenalin pulsing up our veins delivering us to the next enemy attacker. The army had filled every dummy with pig guts to ensure we got our kills and our blood. Every obstacle was overlooked by another officer shouting. We tore the enemy apart with our bayonets then charged to the next with another savage thrust, splattering ourselves with the blood and guts, as lost in the fog of war as it is possible to be in an exercise. By the time we finished we were unsure if we'd imagined it, a near psychosis.

In the aftermath as my head cleared I thought briefly of those Scots Guards in the Falklands, charging up the freezing mountain into the machine gun nests, and what the real thing must be like.

I wondered if I would ever get to experience anything like it again, and how I would react if it was the real thing.

Guard's training culminated in a two week long simulated battle camp. We lived in the field in dug in trenches. Lots of live firing exercises; river crossings with full equipment, our gear wrapped in our ponchos; night time raids on our camp – this all took place in Thetford in Norfolk, near enough to where they filmed the TV series *Dad's Army*. But we were no "Dad's Army"; we were the younger deadlier version.

Over the two weeks in the trenches the NCOs were constantly trying to catch us out with weapons inspections in the middle of the night, or gas attacks while we were eating our first meal for 24 hours. After it was all over the NCOs sat everyone down in a big group and went off in a huddle to decide our fates. The sword of Damocles hung over each and every one of us.

I squeezed through, I will never forget the feeling:

"Jeez I've done it, I'm a Guardsman."

That final day after the battle camp I was filling in a trench when Sergeant Wilson called me from a truck window. To us he was known as Mad Dog Wilson. I was eighteen, he was in his early thirties at the time. He was my platoon sergeant, the man who trained me and I looked up to him. Yes he was very hard but he was fair; a combination I have always responded well to. Ultimately I could owe my life to him and my training. Out of all the instructors I had, he was the one whose memory stayed with me.

"Barry" he roared. I sprinted over, "Well son you've done it. I'm proud of you."

It was a proud, proud moment in my life. He finished with,

"Love me or hate me, you'll never forget me." And he was right. Thirty two years later I've not forgotten him and I never will.

After the battle camp those of us who remained smiled secretly while we worked on parade preparation. We knew we were soon to be Guardsmen.

The last day of being a recruit, we wore our number one dress and had our passing out parade at the Guards Depot. My family turned up to see me become Guardsman Alan Barry. It was a simple good feeling, and I stood to attention in front of my family with great pride.

Chapter 4
GUARDING THE QUEEN

Guardsman Alan Barry was posted to the 2nd Battalion Grenadier Guards stationed in Chelsea Barracks, London. As soon as I arrived at Chelsea, I was immediately posted to the athletics team and I didn't really put on a uniform, well at least not a dress uniform, for my first three months as a Guardsman. When I eventually joined up with Number 2 Company, there were a fair few remarks about my absence. I was billeted to a room with three other guys. They'd all been in the battalion a while and they looked after me.

Barrack room lawyers are soldiers who take it upon themselves to make sure new recruits know their place. In Chelsea Barracks they taught us our place through violence. Thankfully the first evening they came looking for me I was out of barracks. Later on when I got back my roommates warned me I was being hunted. Luckily that night the fourth bed in our room was empty, that Guardsman had a girlfriend and spent most nights out of barracks. I snuck into his bed and covered my head, when they came back asking where I was, my roommates repeated that nobody had seen me.

The following time I wasn't so lucky, they dragged me up to the ablutions as we called them. They gave me a few decent digs. The third time was a couple of days later. Four of them beat the daylights out of me. I got back to my bed and I thought, I'm not having this and, having identified their leader, I went into his room while he was asleep and I smashed a broom stick over his back. He sprung up and hit me and I hit him back. He sneered at me,

"You're dead sprog." Sprog was the nickname given to all the new guys.

I nodded my agreement with him,

"You'll need to kill me, because if you come for me again and don't kill me, I'll definitely be back, so you best sleep with one eye open. I know you're the ring leader and I'm not taking this shit again."

This violent altercation seemed to satisfy something in him as his eyes glinted, and neither he nor his cohorts ever came for me again. Others were not so lucky. One chap was called "football head", due to him continually getting his head kicked in. Other new recruits were nailed into boxes overnight, some hung outside the windows in mattress covers. I never took part in any of this, it sickened me. I'm not sure why, but beating up on the underdog was not something I needed or wanted to be a part of. The sergeants only ever did something about it when it got so bad that they could no longer ignore it.

In Chelsea Barracks there were four weekly guard duties: Tower of London, Windsor Castle, Buckingham Palace, and St James' Palace with Clarence House, where the Queen Mother lived. Clarence House was the easiest. Tower of London was a doddle, or it was viewed as a pleasant guard duty anyway. On guard duty we did two hours on stag, as we called it, four hours off and 24 hour shifts. For the four hours off we mostly spent them in the barrack room; we'd sleep or watch TV. We fought the boredom with the latest video releases, books or eating in the canteen. We never needed to fight anything else, the job was mostly ceremonial.

I recall vividly the first time I mounted guard at Buckingham Palace, marching out of Wellington Barracks with the regimental colours in front and the band playing The British Grenadiers, the sergeant telling us:

"Now lads, chins up, this is your regimental march."

Tourists looked on admiringly taking our photos. I was just nineteen and I was still only 5'8", but nevertheless I felt ten feet tall.

While on Windsor Castle Guard Duty one beautiful morning, Her Majesty the Queen was out strolling whilst having a chat with a member of her staff, very close to number six post behind her private residence. Her Majesty looked straight at me and made eye contact as I presented arms. This was one of the proudest moments of my life. After all, the Grenadiers are her personal Household Troops, their allegiance sworn to protect the monarch and her family.

Once on the Old Guard at Buckingham Palace, I found myself in some discomfort with my newly issued, very tight bearskin. Warrant Officer 1(WO1) Barry Inglis was in charge of drill on the other guard, New Guard. Everyone called him Julio behind his back because of the famous singer Julio Iglesias at the time. We, the Old Guard, had finished our duty and were set to march out. I was always on the left flank, front rank. My bearskin was excruciatingly tight and I was in a lot of pain. I'd just come off sentry duty, so I had been wearing it for over two hours, and it was killing me. I quickly flicked my head to alleviate the pressure for a millisecond. WO1 Ingles marched from the New Guard across the square up behind me and whispered in my ear.

"What's your name?"

I told him "Guardsman Barry Sir"

He marched over to my sergeant of the guard and spoke to him. When we arrived back in barracks I was informed I'd been seen flinching, and put on report for moving on Royal Guard. I was marched in front of the Regimental Sergeant Major, the RSM, who roared at me and there was nothing I could say. I was jailed for 24 hours and put on restriction of privileges for seven days. The next time I was back on guard at Buckingham Palace, WO1 Barry "Julio" Inglis marched up to me and in one of those strange confusing questions so beloved of people in authority asked,

"Guardsman Barry, my favourite Guardsman, why do I like you so much?"

I genuinely hadn't a clue. "I don't know sir." I replied.

"What's my first name?" he asked.

I replied again slightly bewildered, "I don't know Sir." At that stage I had no idea who he was.

"When we dismount guard, you'll tell me my first name, and then you'll know why I like you so much."

In the guardroom later I asked Guardsman Nigel Claridge who'd been in for a while,

"What the hell's he talking about? What's his first name?"

"Barry Ingles, that's what Julio is going on about Barry."

And he laughed. I got to know Nigel Claridge's sense of humour well as we became good mates in the battalion. That first time though I didn't laugh, but I had an idea I thought might get me a bit of respect. After we dismounted guard WO1 Ingles came up to me and asked again,

"What's my first name?"

I stood to attention and in a very loud voice I said "Julio Sir"

That was it, jailed again. Another week of no privileges, even the RSM while he was screaming at me later was trying hard to stifle a smile. I've not been to many regimental reunions since, but I went to one about fifteen years ago. The non-coms remembered the incident and were still laughing about it.

Another Warrant Officer dubbed Slimy Young was completely mad. One evening as I was minding my own business walking back to my billet, Slimy approached me and ordered me to name ten battle honours from the regimental colour. I couldn't, so he punched me quite beautifully into the stomach and jailed me; he was drunk and had just come from the Sergeant's mess. Funny moments looking back, postcards compared to what was to come.

The stark contrast in the Grenadiers was one minute being ceremonial Guardsmen and then suddenly being thrust into action. There were a couple of unusual duties. When Rajiv Ghandi came to London, we were deployed to Heathrow on patrol to provide security and help the police. In those days the police were not armed. The powers that be were rightly worried the poor man would be assassinated, and he was years later back in India.

I am not sure people realise how close we were to being deployed when the 1985 Brixton riots were taking place. We'd just finished our Northern Ireland training consisting mostly of riot tactics, thus we were considered the best placed to go in. We were called back to the barracks on that Saturday night during the worst of the rioting and put on standby; we were going in if the police lost further control.

At the time if they'd sent the Grenadier Guards to Brixton, there would have been serious trouble. Back in the day, black guys were not permitted in the regiment. They simply were not allowed in. If you were a black person you could not join the Guards. How they got away with it for so long, I don't know. If you had a sun tan you could not join the Guards. It was exceptionally racist at the time. Now you even have a soldier in the Scots Guard wearing a turban, as it should be. The Grenadiers were able to get away with it because of tradition and history, the usual sticks to enforce unwritten rules. It was not until the mid-80s when Prince Charles was reviewing the trooping of the colour and famously decried the lack of coloured Guardsmen that the regiment was opened up, although it still took years.

Our officers were recruited from the elite of society. Even young men whose fathers had done well in business and been fortunate to afford a good private school, they could still not join the Guards as officers. They would have needed a double barrelled surname and a private income outside of the army salary. There was not much difference between that system and purchasing your commission back in the day. Hence our officers came almost exclusively from Eton and Harrow. There was one officer who was brilliant. He was an ex-Selous scout from the Rhodesian Army. Probably the best officer I ever had, he was incredible and I was fortunate to have him as my platoon commander in Northern Ireland. They were not bad guys, the double barrels. Most of them were really in it for the prestige before going into the City of London. That was the impression we had anyway. The young ones scared us as they never seemed to quite grasp the gravity of military leadership. The career officers were excellent. We had very experienced NCO's and the smarter officers used them. This is normally the way, it's a well known fact that throughout the history of the British army that a smart officer will realise he has a platoon sergeant with possible ten years plus experience and potentially a couple of active service tours under his belt. A smart NCO will guide his Officer into making a decision and that is the way it should be so as the chain of command is never compromised

Chapter 5
LIMITED LINES OF SIGHT

Northern Ireland, January 1986
Towards the end of 1985, 2nd Battalion was informed that we were being deployed to Northern Ireland. The Troubles were in full tumult, with soldiers regularly being killed in action. Before we went, we did the specially designed Northern Ireland Training. It mainly consisted of riot tactics with some classes on urban patrol. The training area was a replica Derry City, murals on the walls, burnt out cars, tight alleys and limited lines of site. In preparation we drilled street patrols and checkpoints in hostile terrain. Everything was done to mimic Northern Ireland, to get us used to what we would face over there. We were put into a security base at the side of replica Derry, living there just like we would be when we got over to Northern Ireland.

During riot training, the army, with its customary sense of humour, used actors and fake rioters from a regiment that didn't like us. In the Grenadiers' case it was the Parachute Regiment. Our arch rivals, dressed in civvies threw petrol bombs and stones at us, and generally simulated a riot. While they were causing a commotion, we worked on riot tactics. Our standard formation was a slow moving Saracen[4] or Green Giant in the middle, Guardsmen either side with the long riot shields, and behind the formation were Guardsmen with fire extinguishers and rifles covering us. It was like a modern day Roman legion cohort[5]. The simulations were pretty lifelike up to, but not including, firing rubber bullets into the rioters. I was known to be pretty quick, a fast runner, and I was put in the snatch squad which peeled off the main group, or went from behind the main body of the riot, to grab the leaders or the most troublesome. When we eventually arrived in Northern Ireland

4 The FV603 Saracen is a six-wheeled armoured personnel carrier built by Alvis and used by the British Army
5 Definition

we were in a couple of riots. One particular riot in Portadown involved Protestants incensed with the recently signed Anglo Irish Agreement.

The following year in the middle of a particularly dirty riot, petrol bombs raining down on us, a fellow Guardsman turned to me squinting his eyes and through smoke and sticky air said, "They never told us about this in the brochures, all I saw was wind surfing and rock climbing." So we had a laugh. Smoke everywhere, screaming and yelling, rubber bullets going off. The brochure couldn't have captured the glamour as there was none; Northern Ireland felt like going to war in the roughest part of the UK, and like going to war in a parallel universe. Zero glamour.

January 1986 the Grenadier Guards 2nd Battalion was stationed to Ballykelly, Limavady, County Tyrone. Northern Ireland was a bemusing experience for me. I am not sure what I expected but it was not what I got. I thought of myself as British but with a lot of time for the Irish, I reckoned I would be feted by both sides, or something like that, not exactly carried aloft up the Falls and down the Shankhill, but recognised as someone with a balanced outlook. I was, I realise now, delusional.

The first day we were patrolling through the Head of the Town in Strabane. At the time Strabane was dubbed the most bombed town in Northern Ireland, a badge of sorts. I was crouched down in a front garden behind a small typical Northern Ireland red brick wall. The owner opened the front door and I greeted him politely. I think I said "Good morning." In my slightly Brummie accent,

"Fuck of ye Brit bastard", was his reply, which made me laugh. That day I was most definitely English. Similarly the day I got off a school bus, after I'd just finished searching it up and down for a suspect. My ears were ringing with "fuck off ye Brit Bastard", and unbeknownst to me, my back was covered in fifty school boys' phlegm and spit, yeah I was British that day as well.

Whilst we were stationed in Strabane, there was a Catholic secondary school in the town. Often when we sped past, the boys – some of them not that much younger than us – would miraculously appear with stones and bricks and hurl them at us. Tyrone was not exactly a barrel of laughs; we felt surrounded. It was a generally oppressive atmosphere so any chance at some levity was grasped, and when I suggested to the rest of my brick that we have a wee bit of a laugh, everyone was up for it.

We pulled an Irish national flag, a tricolour, from a lamppost in a Nationalist estate and attached it to a broom stick. Already laughing ourselves half sick, we drove our Land Rover to the school and stopped outside. We waved the big garish green, white and gold flag from the open roof hatch. The boys came running out ready to stone us and froze, I can still see them rooted to the spot, mouths agape, all trying to figure out what they were looking at. For as long as I live I will remember their astonished faces as the thoughts fled across them,

"Is it the Irish Army?"

"Is it an invasion?"

"Did the IRA nick it?"

Then just as the spell was wearing off, we opened up the hatches and started laughing and shouting at them and giving them the one finger salute. The young lads roared back, chased to the gate to pelt us with the ever-present stones.

Both sides went back to their positions in the trenches. The battle was rejoined.

Chapter 6
RHYME OR REASON?

Northern Ireland makes you choose every day – choose where you're from, if you're Catholic or Protestant. Dealing with the Ulster Defence Regiment (UDR) was very uncomfortable for me. I regarded them as thugs in uniform. They were outright sectarian in their behaviour and this rankled with me. I saw myself as a British soldier and there to do a job. This is what soldiers tend to say and feel about their circumstances the world over. Our focus on our job and our duty, as well as adherence to the training, gets us through. It also prevents situations from descending into complete chaos. When soldiers are involved in the politics, you are going to have worse problems – the UDR being a case in point.

It was a thick summer's night during the 1986 World Cup and Northern Ireland had been playing. We were on a checkpoint in Country Tyrone, between the towns of Six Mile Cross and Five Mile Town. We were with some UDR and two Royal Ulster Constabulary (RUC) Officers. They were breathalysing drivers as they came through the checkpoint. The RUC had pulled over two drivers who'd failed the breathalyser. Soon after, another quite clearly inebriated man pulled up. The UDR and RUC laughed and joked with him and waved him on.

I asked "Why'd you wave him on?"

"Well he's on our side."

"What do you mean?"

"He's a Protestant."

"Well what about those two over there?" I asked.

"They're Fenians[6]", was the response. I thought to myself: they've all taken the risk drinking and driving, they've all broken the law.

"That's not right." Was my reply.

---

6 Catholic Nationalists

"What do you mean that's not right? They're Fenians." He replied incredulously.

"You can't do that. Just because someone is a Protestant doesn't give you a reason to let them off. My father is an Irish Catholic and he could be one of those two guys just as easy." was my response.

"That's different." He said.

"No, not having it, you either bag everybody or nobody, but you can't just arrest someone depending on whether they're a Catholic or a Protestant."

"Well that's the way it is here." He retorted, upping the bullying ante. I hate bullies.

"Listen lads that's not going to work, either you take them all in or you let those two go, we are all here risking our necks and we are not here to support blatant sectarianism."

"Really, is that right?" Was his reply.

I stood my ground, the three guys in my brick all backed me. The UDR let the two Catholics go. Kind of sums up something that was wrong with Northern Ireland, why not arrest all of them? They were all way over the limit.

A complaint was handed in and I was spoken to the next day by my Platoon Commander,

"You know your problem Barry, you think too much. We are here to do a job, we are not here to get involved in local politics." There is never any point in answering back to an officer in the Guards.

Northern Ireland kept asking me the same question: "Where are you from?" Each time I answered I was a little bit more certain.

Another lovely summer's evening at a border checkpoint on the way through Aughnacloy to Omagh, a route used by a lot of Southern cars as a short cut to Donegal. I was in the centre sanger[7] with an RUC officer and my job was to check

7 A sanger is a protected sentry post, normally located around the perimeter of a base. Its main function is to provide early warning of enemy/terrorist activity/attack in order to protect forces both within the base and those deployed within sight of the Sanger.

documents. The soldier in the front sanger covered the border with a machine gun and would sound a buzzer to tell us when there was a car approaching from the Republic. The front sanger radioed the plates to Central Intelligence to run through the system. If a car had been registered to a known player or involved in an incident, we would pull them over. Each soldier had Aide Memoires, like the American deck of cards in the Iraq Wars with a list of known players. Aide Memoires were a list of men and women connected with known terrorist organisations. Much like a Filofax, giving details of their history, a picture, names and aliases.

A Ford Granada estate, big family car with a mother, father and two children, pulled up with the old Southern Irish red number plates. As my eyes scanned the massive pink driving license, I noticed that the father was from Artane in Dublin.

"O you're from Artane are you?"

The man took a second or two to react, did a double take, and then answered,

"Yeah I am." He replied still looking puzzled.

"Do you know the Grove disco?"

"Course I do."

"I used to go to the Grove disco there in Clontarf when I was a teenager."

We had a bit of a chat about going to the Grove as youngsters. I stood there with my Grenadier's beret and a sidearm, chatting to him about Artane and the famous alternative North Dublin music club. The whole situation was pretty alternative alright. The father got over the shock and chatted amiably for a few minutes. I let him on his way, with a word of caution not to stop in Omagh; Omagh was not advisable for anyone with a Southern reg.

When I returned to the centre sanger the RUC officer in his fly green uniform said nothing at first, but couldn't hold it in. With his two thumbs pinned under his shoulders, looking at me like a peacock he asked,

"So are you Irish then?"

"Yeah I'm Irish." I am not sure I had ever really said it before, I was certainly never sure of it before.

"What's your surname?"

"Barry." A very important question in Northern Ireland, as it indicates which religious background you have.

"So you're a Catholic?" The crux.

"Yeah what's that got to do with anything?" I asked ever so slightly tensing.

"I just find it strange that you are in the British Army?"

I was taken aback by this.

"What's that supposed to mean? I grew up in Britain and I wanted to be a soldier, so I joined the best regiment in the British Army."

"What's more," I insisted, "down South nobody ever asks: are you a Catholic or a Protestant? Both live in harmony."

I couldn't stop myself then, I was only young, I gave him my whole speech.

"In Phoenix Park in Dublin there's a memorial to 375,000 Irish soldiers who fought in the British Army and the 50,000 who died fighting in the First World War. Out of a population of three million people, that is a significant number of men. And most of those were Catholics."

I thought I was on a roll so I kept going,

"If you were ever to set one foot out of Northern Ireland into England, you would be treated as well or as badly as any other Paddy. No one's bothered that you're a loyal Protestant who loves the Queen. If there's a bombing and you're rounded up, I promise you'll be treated as a Paddy or a Mick, don't doubt it. To the average Brummie or Cockney, you're just a Mick."

He didn't say much else after that.

My brick used a starburst formation whenever we left our barracks on patrol, each of us sprinting out and running in different directions. Exiting the base is when you're the most vulnerable, or at least it is the one thing the enemy knows you have to do. One day leaving Sion Mills Barracks in Tyrone on patrol, I saw a young man I'd previously noticed earlier that week. He was standing at the exact same corner. I was suspicious, reckoned we were being dicked by the IRA.[8]

We made our way down the road in standard two by two formation; two men one side and two on the other, with the final Guardsman responsible for guarding the rear. While I was approaching the suspect, my radio sounded and startled him. He sprinted away, we gave pursuit. The suspect ran into a hair dressing salon where we cut him off and caught him. Unbeknownst to either of us, Violet, the woman I would later marry, was the manager of that salon.

I interviewed the suspect in the salon; he had difficulty speaking due to his shy disposition. I questioned him, taking down his details. It turned out he was a no one, not what we called a player, just a local unemployed lad with nothing to do, wiling away his time. The manager of the salon, Violet, vouched for the young man.

In March 1986 two friends of mine died in very tragic circumstances. I'd joined up with Paul "Ronald" McDonald from Manchester; he'd been back squaded for something or other in basic training but he'd caught back up and joined the 2nd Battalion. Then there was Brian "Virgil" Hughes from Chester, a particularly good mate of mine. They were in the QRF on that fateful evening, the Quick Reaction Force, a group within the regiment tasked with reacting to any immediate danger. That awful day a warning came in, intruders had been spotted inside our base and the QRF was dispatched. Virgil and Ronald were in the back of the Land Rover that sped to the location.

The main coastal Belfast to Derry rail line ran through the bottom of our base. The QRF Land Rover mounted the railway tracks in pursuit, the intruders escaped and the QRF Land Rover got jammed and stuck on the tracks. My description

---

8 Dicked was when the IRA had someone watching us, spying on us, trying to identify patterns in our behaviour. Once identified, the IRA would then use a sniper or an IED or a car bomb to ambush and try to kill us. Being dicked was what we called their reconnaissance gathering missions.

separates a sequence of events that all happened virtually simultaneously. Mangled into a blur, the driver, the impending train, the charging heavy metal, the train engulfing the Land Rover then catapulting it into mid-air. Those Land Rovers had no back doors to allow for an easy exit in an emergency.

The ferocity of the train's impact hurled Guardsman Hughes and Guardsman McDonald out the back of the Land Rover. The barrel of McDonald's SLR[9] went straight through Virgil, right through his abdomen. McDonald was killed instantly. Virgil had massive internal injuries and he died a few days later. The surgeon told our platoon commander that the only reason Virgil had survived for so long was his physical fitness. I was badly affected by this. They were so young, like I was. Just kids. Virgil was blond and had blue eyes, with an amazing complexion so we nicknamed him Virgil after Thunderbirds. I still remember them both. I understood their lives but I found it hard to make sense of their deaths. In a murderous land, accidents seem even more out of place. Fruitless looking for rhyme or reason.

We were on patrol right on the border beside Strabane not far from Clady. We'd been doing a route clearance down a road somewhere in the midst of County Tyrone and we'd stopped to have tea. The British Army runs on tea. There we were having a cup of tea at the side of a culvert at the bottom of a little bank, when behind us the dirt exploded followed by a roar; simultaneous to this we dropped into our positions, and instantaneously began a section attack on the farm building at the top of the ridge where we'd been fired upon from. I remember knowing to do this immediately without thinking.

"Move" we shouted.

Two moved up, the other two giving covering fire. Then they ascended while the front two provided covering fire. At all times fire was being laid down on the enemy position. We used a magazine each sprinting up the ridge. When we reached the

---

9 SLR Self-Loading Rifle has a magazine of 20 rounds of 7.62 mm, and was the standard British Army Infantry Assault Rifle.

top there was no one there. We'd been fired on by an M-60[10], an American heavy machine gun, we found some shell cartridges in the grass on top of the ridge.

After all the adrenalin and commotion had died down, the first thing that came to mind was the Bayonet Assault Course. I'd wondered since that day in basic training what it would feel like to be involved in combat. I'd asked myself almost every day, what would I do? How would I react? That day I got my answer. I did what I'd been trained to do, we all did. We didn't need to think, training told us what to do, focused us on the job.

The lingering thought was of my instructors making us go through that Godforsaken Bayonet Course.

They really did know what they were doing.

---

10 M-60 GPMG was the American General Purpose Machine Gun 7.62 Calibre. Rate of fire 675 rounds per minute.

Chapter 7

HARD HAT AND SOFT HAT

I found it difficult to tolerate the apartheid regime in Northern Ireland, turning a blind eye to the Ulster Defence Regiment (UDR). For myself, the most difficult aspect of the initial period in Northern Ireland was getting used to working alongside the Unionist security forces who dominated the country. I sometimes found it awkward guarding Orangemen as my realisation of my Irishness grew. I say all these things in hindsight, but in truth my Irish identity did not matter to the job at hand and I was given more and varied responsibilities as time went on. I was a British Soldier, there to fight terrorists and keep peace in Northern Ireland, which is what I told myself and what I believed most days. Perhaps in moments of doubt, I think back and wonder was the reality the opposite. Had I just been there like all British Soldiers to maintain an acceptable level of violence?

Wherever the British Army see active service, they try and adopt a hard hat and a soft hat status. When the conflict is over they put on their berets in an attempt to further deflate the conflict, and with it the levels of tension and confrontation with the locals. The British Army arrived in Northern Ireland with the berets and the process worked in reverse. As far as I am concerned, there were two real antagonists in Northern Ireland: the IRA and the Unionists. The violence of the IRA arose out of the blatant sectarianism of the Protestant Unionist agenda. When I went there as a professional soldier, I went there for a reason: because it was my duty. I certainly did not go there because I believed the six counties should be part of the United Kingdom, but I accept there is not much we can do about it anymore. It's a catch 22 situation and in my view only time and healing can bring peace.

Some of the Protestants I met in Northern Ireland were bigots. They were closed minded and bunkered into their own little community. Nowadays they still blatantly antagonise the Catholic population with their marching. The Orange Order is basically the Ku Klux Klan of the North. As a British soldier I did not want to believe that I was there in any capacity to protect any type of bigotry.

I admit to not really knowing a great deal about the North before I arrived; the only thing my father had said to me was, "Son they are not like us, don't mix them up with the people you've met in Dublin."

It was being there that opened up my eyes to it. I could not believe the rampant sectarian antagonism. It awakened in me an awareness of my Irish identity that has remained with me. While some of us Guardsmen didn't much like it, to many of the others it was just a job. The average British soldier did not want to be there and could not understand why we were there. The soldier was stuck in the middle with a target on his back. Unlike my fellow Guardsmen, who'd pretty much spent their whole lives in Britain, I'd been to Ireland and my parents were Irish. I didn't like what I was seeing. I didn't like seeing Catholics being treated as second class citizens, very much as they'd been treated for hundreds of years.

It is important to remember that the British Army went in there to protect the Catholic population from the Special Bs; a quasi-military reserve force of thugs in uniform. When the Special Bs were disbanded most of them moved into the Ulster Defence Regiment. The UDR was rumoured to be riddled with members of the UVF and other sectarian right wing Protestant groups. I did meet very decent Protestants, but they were few and far between in my military dealings there.

Forgive me for being baffled recently by the tributes that poured in at the death of Ian Paisley. That man caused nothing but havoc in Northern Ireland. This is the man that interrupted Pope John Paul II's speech to the European Parliament in 1988 with an anti-papist diatribe, shouting and holding up posters calling the Pope an antichrist: not exactly the actions of a man of peace.

I continued to grapple with my nationality and person. I could understand more and more why the Catholics had risen up against the oppressive regime, but I still believed in what

I was doing. Growing up in Birmingham I remembered well the IRA's Birmingham Pub Bombings, I'll certainly never forget them.

In Northern Ireland it was apparent the Catholics were educating themselves. As an ex-British soldier I've respect for Martin McGuinness, I would like to shake his hand if I ever met him, and I hope he would shake mine. McGuinness has proven to be a true statesman. I say this as someone who would not have hesitated in giving him the *Good News* back in the 80s and would have expected the same treatment from him. Thankfully the war is over and it's down to leaders like McGuinness and the late David Irvine – men who took up arms for what they believed in and then turned to the path of peace and reconciliation. They deserve respect.

My feelings on being Irish and being in the British Army have always been difficult. Somehow the contradictory nature of the two feelings embodies who I am. Like many Irish in Ireland maybe I am partly West Brit. Who knows? My dual loyalty was confirmed on the Queen's 2011 historic visit to Dublin: a very proud day for Ireland and Britain, and long overdue.

I am asked every year or two, normally when someone finds out a little bit about my past,

"How could you, being Irish, go to Northern Ireland and serve as a British Soldier?"

My answer changes or evolves each time but I tend to reply,

"Well, if you are asking me do I believe that Northern Ireland is British, I would say no, I don't. I would love to see a united Ireland one day, but I didn't go there to defend Northern Ireland as a British territory, I went to fight terrorism and protect the people, including the Nationalists."

It was my job.

I spent a year based in Limavady, but saying that I could be in Strabane, Castle Derg or Aughnacloy. They moved us where they needed us. I was put into the intelligence unit that formed part of Headquarters Company in the battalion. We moved about the North in a variety of civilian disguises. It was gulp gulp but I liked it, I think we all did. My job was to drive and surveil. The battalion had a shortage of drivers so this suited me as the job was far more interesting than being in a rifle platoon. The Intelligence Cell performed a wide variety of duties: some mundane like escorting army wives out shopping, ensuring they were safe; some more serious like keeping an eye on undercover lorries filled with British soldiers.

The following week we could be back inside the barracks in uniform, but once we joined the Int Cell we no longer went out on standard foot patrol. No further foot patrol was to ensure we were sufficiently demilitarised when we were out and about undercover, that we didn't come across as soldiers; we had to loosen up our bones, watch how we held ourselves, our gait.

In my new company, being able to drive, I was given a job driving unmarked cars and transit vans. Normally in these unmarked vehicles there would be two of us tooled up, each armed with a Browning pistol and maybe a sub machine gun, driving around the Province carrying out surveillance and ferrying dignitaries.

A patrol might radio with a grid reference, we'd take the transit vans with civilian plates into bandit country, this could be anywhere and we'd extract the patrol units, particularly when the dark gloomy Northern Irish weather had come down and the helicopters could not fly. Doing that job I was always on edge. This was around the time of the horrific incident when the two corporals, David Howes and Derek Wood, found themselves trapped by a funeral procession. The two corporals were dragged out of their car and murdered in Belfast, their bodies found dumped in a waste land. None of us will ever forget those images. I knew it was a risky post, and I knew what could happen to me. I just got on with it like everybody else. I remember one dark winter's night coming back from the airport, taking a short cut along the Glenshane Pass, near Coleraine and seeing a torch being flashed up ahead. For a split second I thought,

"Fuck, an IRA checkpoint."

The IRA frequently set up their own checkpoints in remote areas as a show of force.

I cocked my weapon. I was not going down without a fight. We all knew what happened if the IRA caught us: tortured to death, our bodies dumped and never found. Turned out to be a man whose car had broken down, bizarre normality. My heart was in my mouth, but I swallowed it and I lived another day hand on weapon.

Chapter 8
MONSTERS IN THE NIGHT

Everyone knew everything and everybody in the North. We all knew that "yer man" was a part time RUC officer, as well as a cattle farmer in Tyrone. The man in the street knew that "yer man" didn't always carry his weapon, that he was an obvious target walking around his farm. Everybody in Northern Ireland always knew who'd killed whom. It was in the air and the longer you were there the easier it became to decipher. Didn't make the place any less dangerous – the opposite in fact.

As well as driving, the new job meant a good deal of surveillance. It was not beyond the realms of possibility we could be nestled in a lovely comfortable Ulster bush for two days, in the thick, damp, cold air, watching said part time RUC officer's farm house. There could have been four of us, three asleep one on stag, working off an Army Intelligence tip. We could have been fully armed waiting to see a van pulling up, to see armed known players getting out and then taking them out if needed.

That would have been bad enough, but there were worse things out there. One afternoon on a lurk[11] somewhere in deepest darkest County Tyrone, we were observing a farm house belonging to another part time RUC officer. There was a whole platoon surveilling from various hidden positions.

My brick were inside a small coppice, a wooded area. One of us on stag, three asleep. Whilst I was asleep in my sleeping bag, head resting against my Bergen[12], I was disturbed by a rustling somewhere under my head sufficient to wake me up. There was something moving inside my Bergen. I thought to myself, "Jesus Christ what is that?" I knew fine well what it was, but I didn't want to know, and I certainly didn't want to have to look at it. But I had no choice, I opened the Bergen and looking right into

11 A lurk was our version of a stake out, a surveillance operation.
12 A rucksack.

39

my eyes was a gigantic farm rat, a thing was the size of a cat, just staring at me and eating my rations. An East Tyrone rat.

If I'd jumped up as I wanted to that would have compromised the mission, nobody knew we were there. So I got a hold of myself and tipped the Bergen upside down. The rat ran off. It had eaten its way into my Bergen to get at my rations. We were there for 48 hours and when you are in a situation like that you don't ever move outside your location. You urinate in bags and so on. Ever since then I have an absolute phobia of rats.

In 1986 I was on an escort duty when we arrived into a barracks to grab something to eat. As always before we entered the mess, we unloaded our weapon and cleared the action. I bumped into a corporal and a sergeant I knew from guard duty at Buckingham Palace, they sat opposite and chatted while my fellow Recce Platoon member and I ate in silence.

My Browning was in my shoulder holster.

The two NCOs were deep in conversation about the Browning. The Sergeant I knew asked me could he borrow my weapon. When an NCO asks you for something you give it to them, end of. They were discussing the pros and cons of half cocking a Browning and the speed advantage this gives you. The disadvantage being the Browning is the easiest weapon to have a negligent discharge with, an ND. I only know all this in hindsight I was not really paying attention to them at the time. I handed the weapon over and continued eating.

While the corporal was talking he actually half-cocked the weapon and unbeknownst to me put a round in the chamber. The sergeant, not knowing this either, handed the weapon back to me, I foolishly saw the hammer was back and fired the weapon; there was an almighty bang, the bullet penetrated the table and went through my colleague's groin, luckily clean through. I'd shot him at point blank range. For micro seconds I thought I'd killed him. It was my weapon, I was responsible for it, irrespective of who loaded it. Thankfully it was a 9ml round and it went straight through at close range. Because the pistol was pointing down nobody was severely hurt, although it'd missed his testicles by inches.

I was in deep shit. I was charged with all sorts and the incident was investigated by the military police to find out whether anybody had had a psychotic episode. In the end I thought I was lucky. I was charged with having a negligent discharge and fined a month's salary, my colleague was back on duty in a couple of months and kept his testicles.

I was back on duty within a few weeks armed with my Browning. When you are carrying around loaded weapons accidents do happen. I wasn't the only soldier to have an ND that year, and as a good friend from the battalion said to me only recently, I wasn't the last.

A few years later in another land far far away from the alleys and hedgerows of Northern Ireland, I was caught in the middle of something more serious and I had to take someone down. But that is another story for another day and another book.

Years later those incidents would come back to haunt me. The truth is they never left me. What really throws me to this day, is the PTSD inside me lying latent. Or partially latent, it infused everything I did one way or another for the next twenty years and dictated my behaviour, despite me being unaware of it and appearing, on the surface at least, perfectly healthy.

I was fearless in those days. Nothing bothered me. Why? Well I was to find out later why. Suffice to say that it should have been a cause for concern, but in truth it never even occurred to me.

I'd like to ask my old self, is it normal at 24 to shoot a man? Is it normal to see your friends killed in front of you? But I can't.

Chapter 9

THE FORGOTTEN WARS

My grandfather John Barry, my Dad's father, was in the old IRA, the IRB[13]. A tailor by profession, he's buried in Glasnevin. He died the same year I was born, so unfortunately I have no memories of him. Grandfather Barry was on crutches his whole life as he suffered from Polio and thus had very weak legs. Grandfather Barry worked for the IRB in the 1916 uprising when he was very young. They had him running messages around Dublin because he didn't look like a threat. He looked like an inoffensive character and he was able to move about Dublin City relatively un-harassed. Messengers like my grandfather had to memorise and then destroy the messages. Unfortunately this meant that if they were caught they would be tortured to get the information. Sean MacDiarmada, one of the executed leaders of the Rising, also suffered from polio. Neither man allowed the polio to get in the way of his bravery. For years after the Rising, people in the neighbourhood, who were unaware of the Polio, told tales of how Grandfather Barry had been shot in the leg in the "Rising", after each telling the story got better and better like all classic Irish tales. My Dad would always tell me,

"That was the old IRA back then son."

My mum's grandfather Patrick Nolan was a Scots Guardsman who fought in the Boer War. He was involved in two campaigns: Cape Colony and Orange Free State. He was awarded the Queen's South Africa medal in 1902 and discharged in 1906. When he returned from South Africa Patrick Nolan met my great grandmother, an O'Toole from County Wicklow, and they married. They lived their years off Dorset Street, at 61 Lower Wellington Street, Dublin. Although he'd already been a professional soldier

13 Irish Republican Brotherhood 1858-1924

he re-enlisted for the First World War in the Middlesex Regiment in 1914. One can only imagine what he witnessed but whatever he saw and felt he never recovered. When he returned he was not the same. Before he went he had been a very loving caring man, a well-disciplined man. After his return he suffered from extreme bouts of anger and whatever happiness he'd carried inside of him had been extinguished on Belgian fields. He never spoke about it and, like many First World War vets, he took to the bottle.

One normal day when he came home with a few drinks on him the rage seized him. He snatched his First World War medals off the fireplace and hurled them into the fire. They were never recovered. I have no idea how he handled the homecoming many Irish had, coming back to an island riven and ready to revolt. Dublin was not as welcoming to a British soldier as when he left it. Although he was never good with people he worked as a hand craft tailor in Arnotts the department store in Dublin until 1946 when he passed away.

My great grandmother Julia was a business woman and ran the family shop. She kept guns under the floorboards for the IRA during the 1920s. The Black and Tans would come into the shop in Dublin, see the picture of her husband in the British Army uniform on the wall and maybe go a little bit easier on her. She was never caught.

Having a grandfather in the IRA and a great grandfather serving in the British Army is part of who I am. These are the myriad thoughts that linger and confuse when one side or the other accuse me of being on the wrong side.

My grandmother loved Michael Collins. We were brought up listening to tales of his daring exploits when we'd come in from school. She grew up with a father who wore the poppy so she and her sisters would always wear lilies just to rile him a little. The lilies are a symbol of remembrance for those who fell in the Easter Rising. Prior to my passing out of the Guards, I was having a look around the regimental gift shop and I found my grandmother a little Scots Guard

Piper to remind her of her father. She broke down when I handed it to her. She also brought a tear to my eye when she said to me,

"He would have been so proud to know his great grandson became a Guardsman."

My nickname within the rugby brotherhood is The Tan and I don't have a problem with this as I guess, in some kind of way, that's what I was except it also helped me to come to terms with my Irish identity. Everyone despised the Black and Tans. Everyone talks about the atrocities they committed. Who were they? They were professional soldiers that survived the First World War. Nowadays historians would explain if anyone asked that the Tans were not all British that some of them were Irish. In fact approximately 20% of the Black and Tans were Irish.

The Black and Tans were not prisoners that had been let out on day release on the proviso they went out and killed Irish people. They weren't lunatics that had been released from the asylum and all the other myths that Irish folklore has come up with. The Black and Tans, like the Auxiliaries, were men that had survived the trenches in the First World War. But of course that in itself would have been enough to kill a man inside. If you shot at them they would shoot back, if you didn't shoot at them they would shoot back. One mad day, in an alleged reprisal for a previous attack on British troops, the Black and Tans burnt Cork City to the ground after going on a crazed rampage throughout the city. They were named after a combination of the uniform that they wore, kaki top with black trousers, and a pack of wild dogs, hunting hounds that formed part of a fox hunt. They came to Ireland from the war and they never stopped fighting. They probably all had PTSD one hundred times worse than anything I could ever imagine.

When I served in the North in what we now call the Forgotten War, the RUC put all the Catholics in one guilty melting pot as IRA or IRA sympathisers. To them, every Catholic was a Republican. I split the two, as far as I was concerned the IRA were distinct and over here; the rest of the Catholic community were over there. Those children that spat all over my back, they were only doing what had been bred into them. Most of them would have gone on to have respectable family lives.

Chapter 10
MIRRORING THE PAST

My new surveillance job in Northern Ireland allowed me a little bit of leeway with my overall physical appearance. I had slightly longer hair, a more dishevelled, scruffy appearance and a fake student ID. Together they got me into Trax Nightclub in Portrush the fateful night I spoke to Violet for the second time – a chance meeting that would impact my life forever. I didn't look like a soldier as I was in my civvies. Soldiers weren't supposed to be in the club and the doormen wouldn't have let me in if they'd known. I was dressed as a student, chatting to her sister when she walked up, I recognised her from our previous encounter when we'd chased the suspect into the hair salon. We got to talking and we were together for the next twenty two years.

Northern Ireland's next twist; Violet was from a staunch Loyalist household. Her father had died many years before in a tragic car accident, but her mother maintained a strong Loyalist ethos in the house. Since it was Northern Ireland, we began seeing each other covertly. While the relationship was not exactly army permitted, the secrecy was definitely more to keep it from her mother. New Year's Eve eight months later, when I invited my new girlfriend Violet over to meet my family in Birmingham, things came to a head and my life changed forever. Violet's mum was appalled her daughter had taken up with a Fenian. A Catholic, Irish Fenian, the worst sort.

"Once a Fenian always a Fenian." Was her comment apparently. So much for my guarding and fighting for Queen and country.

When Violet's mother found out I'd invited her to meet my family she gave her daughter an ultimatum. She told her that if she went to Birmingham she'd never be allowed back into her home. Violet went anyway. She enjoyed the convivial kitchen table atmosphere in my family home with my Nan, my mother, brother and sister. She loved that she was immediately accepted. Meanwhile her mother called the barracks to report that her daughter had been kidnapped by a British Fenian Soldier. We've not had any contact with her since. That was the final decision from her mother, but that's not my story to tell.

Violet's aunt and uncle were wonderful people over the years we were married and always made our family feel welcome. More than anything, they have given our children a link with their Northern Irish roots. I am not sure after all these years I can fully grasp the depth of resolve it requires to maintain the impasse her mother has. Even after all the hurt between Violet and I, I still feel for her as I know what she gave up when she decided we should build a future together.

Northern Ireland is confusing, like being stuck in a room of cracked mirrors, looking over your shoulder at distortions, trying to figure out if the reflections you see are really you. I went back to my regiment, but after that things were different. Violet's mother had phoned the barracks in 1987 and I was transferred. She knew everything about me and my commanding officer felt I had been compromised as a result.

A century old story playing itself out again. Tell young people they cannot be together and they grow closer. More than anything else her mother drove us together, and for that I am grateful as I have three wonderful children and a lot of great memories of the 22 years we spent as a couple.

There I was a serving British soldier in Northern Ireland going out with a local girl. My great grandfather from Maguire's Bridge in Northern Ireland had been a serving Scots Guard when he met my great grandmother: an O'Toole from Wicklow. They fell in love despite her family being staunch Irish Republicans. She wanted to marry him. So they asked her father for his permission.

Her father replied,

"If you marry him, you are disowned from this family."

She chose to get married anyway and her parents never spoke to her again. My great grandmother's dying wish was to be buried in the O'Toole family plot in Kilranelagh Graveyard. Coincidentally the same cemetery as Sam McAllister, the United Irishman leader in the 1798 rebellion, is buried. In the end my great grandmother's brother gave up his place in the family plot to allow his sister to be buried there.

Violet and I were following ghosts, dancing those same steps, except in reverse. My own grandmother couldn't believe the similarities, and yet I think they pleased her somehow, made her happy.

I spent a few more years in the army and I was given an exemplary discharge in 1991.

When I left the army I was a time bomb just waiting to go off.

I'd been out about a year or so, working and selling advertising in a local newspaper in Birmingham, when I bought my first expensive suit. It was a Hugo Boss; all the rage at the time. I'd put it on and felt like a million dollars. Perhaps due to my military training, I've always felt it's important to dress really smartly. Looking smart gives an ever lasting impression – I've constantly wanted to be the best, so looking the best has always been part of that. Maybe I've relaxed a bit now, but I still like to look the part.

When I left the army I was a coiled spring.

A year or so into my time as a civilian, I was out with the sales team. My eldest son had just been born. I was feeling great, wearing my new suit, hitting my targets and believing I'd made it. After a few drinks I left the bar on Broad Street in Birmingham. As I was looking for a taxi, this man came towards me at speed, and another unseen man grabbed me from behind putting his arms around my neck. The front attacker reached to get my wallet from the inside suit jacket pocket. I pulled the attacker in front towards me and smashed my forehead onto his nose with tremendous force. The noise and violence of the impact were horrific. He fell to the ground, blood everywhere; the other mugger tore off as I wrestled with him. The screams of my attacker as he writhed in agony on the ground added to the sense of terror. I was drenched in blood, but all I was bothered about was my Hugo Boss jacket. I thought he'd ripped open my suit pocket. The unfortunate attacker on the ground, his nose obliterated, screaming and screaming.

A crowd gathered and a doorman appeared, he took a quick look around and suggested I make myself scarce.

When I left the military I was a fully trained fighting machine.
I got home that night covered in blood. I hand washed my
lovely blue shirt, everything came out physically but I was shaken
by what I'd done. There had been no decision just reaction. People
would look into my eyes when I was younger and they would
know. I was never aggressive outwardly, but inside I was intense.
I held myself very confidently. If someone tried to mug me now, I
would put up my hands and let them take whatever they wanted.
Now I'd be thinking about the knife sliding into my back. Back
in those days it just didn't occur to me, I never took a step back.
I charged through the whole of the nineties.

It was madness. Or perhaps I was the madness.

I'd had a few drinks that night. But I reacted like my training
taught me.

When I left the army I was back to square one.

Troubled

What did you do in the army Daddy?
Did you fight a war?
I've only seen a few old photos Daddy,
Please, tell me some more.,

I wore a scarlet tunic son,
A bearskin with a plume of white.,
I guarded the Queen in London son,
To make sure she slept safe at night

But did I fight a war son?
Politicians will tell you no.,
But let me tell the facts son,
The truth ,as it was, just so.

I went to a beautiful country son,
That is known as the Emerald Isle.
To the North of the South we young men went,
To a place chocked with hate and bile.

I walked the streets with a rifle son,
The enemy hiding from view,
Behind the hedgerows & in vans they hid,
Their mission, our lives to undo.

They wouldn't come out in the light lad,
They'd only fire from the dark.
Too timid to stand toe to toe son,
A yellow streak was their flags mark.

But how do you define a war son?
Is it bullets bombs and death?
Friends dying from enemy ambushes son?
If it is then my answer is yes.

Yes I fought a war my boy,
Though the government denies it all.
They said we just had some troubles son,
Behind a cracked Irish wall.

But didn't they give you a medal Daddy?
The one with the face of the Queen?
All shiny and Silver, your name on it
A ribbon of purple and green?

They did and it brings back that world son,
When   I fought alongside real men.
It recalls those honest true friendships son,
The likes that I will never find again.

So yes I fought a war son
No matter what the politicians say
I would love those same politicians to pick up a rifle my lad
And be troubled for just one day.

Chapter 11

THE NINETIES CAROUSEL

For years I was an exceptionally confident individual and I never stressed about anything. I was oblivious to hubris or karma or anything else that might have given me even a slight pause for contemplation. After leaving the military I knew I didn't want to be poor. It was the only thing I was certain of. With no formal qualifications all I was actually qualified to do was manual labour. Not going to college had caught up with me, as had the advice of the recruiting officer. He had been 100% correct – I had eventually become bored with my life in the military and I'd never learnt a marketable skill. Not much call for a weapon's expert or a trained soldier back in 1991.

Violet and I moved into a very basic apartment, a little bed sit near the centre of Birmingham. I would never call those early years fun. We were probably forced together by circumstance more than anything. The reality is if Northern Ireland and her mother hadn't disowned her we may have never stayed together. I've always had a strong sense of responsibility so I felt practically wedded to Violet from then on. My first job was as a lorry driver, although I had no intention of driving for a living.

While making a pick up one day I saw a well-dressed man get out of a swanky car. Intrigued, I asked what he did, apparently he was in our sales department. Sales: the best job anyone could get without a formal education. That week I handed in my notice. I remember going back to Violet, to our tiny flat, her working as a hairdresser at the time. I told her what I'd done. She couldn't believe it. Not best pleased.

The following Monday morning I walked around every recruitment agency I could find in the centre of Birmingham. I was offered a job in one agency by an ex-military man who had served in the Royal Signals. I was behind a desk, cold calling people, placing candidates in jobs. It was a great start. I enjoyed the recruitment job, however I was eager to move up.

Next up on the nineties carousel I swung into the world of advertising. I had a company car, and initially everything was great. Travelling all over the UK selling but still driving. I did that for about a year and then moved on to another job with a larger UK based advertising firm, Morgan Crampion. I was an area sales manager, an increased salary, a better car and my own office: in short, a higher profile role. Violet and I got married and bought our first little house. My father paid for our wedding. I was that guy. I was on success autopilot, trajectory unknown.

Then the Black Monday bombshell, the recession came with a very loud bang. Norman Lamont withdrew Sterling from the European Exchange Rate Mechanism, suddenly nobody was advertising. Well that's not completely true: mobile phone companies seemed to be going great guns, car phones were all the rage. One of my clients, a mobile phone company, wanted me to come and work for them. I jumped at the chance.

The first month selling mobile phones, I made four times as much as my previous monthly salary. Violet and I were really on our way to the rest of our lives. A friend worked for Martin Dawes, an aggressive expanding organisation based in the North of England. I knew I could make good money there so I joined them. Going to work for Martin Dawes was one of the best decisions I ever made in my life. They were a well-run organisation and I thoroughly enjoyed working there. I became national account manager. If you were good at what you did you were given a licence to go ahead and do your own deals. I met my best friend, Mark, there. We worked together in a sales team of 130 people. Mark and I consistently shared first and second place in the sales league. We were dealing with big ticket sales, in 1996 I was awarded the largest mobile phone contract ever in the UK with British Gas. I did very well that month, very well indeed. I stayed with Martin Dawes up until 1998, through a total of about four years.

I'd first met Mark when he came up to the West Midlands office for a client meeting. There was an element of competitiveness at first and I am not sure we took to each other in the beginning.

Eventually, we developed a friendship of sorts based on mutual respect more than any closeness. Mark was very good at the office politics. He seemed to have the management wrapped around his little finger. I knew I was already very good at selling and was never overly fond of the political side of the job, preferring to let my record speak for itself.

When Mark left the company he started Anglo Communications. Once his company started to do well, he needed someone he could trust as sales director to push the team, particularly a person who would watch his back. The two of us agreed a deal and I went to work with Mark as the sales director of Anglo Communications. From then on our friendship grew. Anglo Communications was a service provider with 30,000 business to business (B2B) subscribers and we had a licence to sell Vodafone and Cellnet (which later became O2). B2B customers spend far more than private customers. Our largest client was McNicholas Construction, they had 750 phones with us. Our head office was in Hampshire. We had a five person sales team and Mark as MD. We were small and very nimble. I spent the next five years selling, making pots of cash and enjoying life. I was earning £20k a month by the end. I was always number one and developed into the stereotype of the nineties sales man: good, brash and very arrogant.

As the nineties ticked on living in England began to bring us down. Despite us living in an upmarket area, our family home was burgled three times in a relatively short space of time. The second time, when Violet came home the burglars were still in the house. The third time they stole my alloy wheels and tyres off my BMW. The car was discovered early one morning at the front of the house on bricks, by a neighbour walking his dog.

We knew we needed to change, but go where?

Chapter 12

THE DALKEY DREAM

Around the time of the burglaries Violet and I were over at the Rose of Tralee on a jolly and missed our ferry home. We took a drive through Dalkey and ended up staying the night there; both of us smiling and musing on how lovely it would be to live in Dalkey. We fell in love with Ireland all over again. Ireland always made us feel like we were home, and we were very enamoured with our stay. Violet and I were both Irish and we could feel the allure of Ireland. Everything back in England seemed more impersonal, harsher and disparate. All the signs were telling us to go home. Ireland seemed easier, rosier and of course smaller. We were less likely to get lost. And most of all we wanted our children to grow up in Ireland.

So we moved to Ireland.

Arriving in Ireland in 1997, I would love to tell you we did everything right, but that would be a lie. For my children, for all of us it was beautiful – great schools and fantastic quality of life. We had pots of cash and life in South Dublin is always easier with pots of cash. I am ashamed to say we got caught up in those heady days somewhat, although we never quite developed the kamikaze approach to property portfolios that many other Irish did. For Violet and I, it was hard to get our head around how a normal everyday Joe could end up owing anybody 23 million. The very thought of paying those exorbitant amounts for property terrified us. We put our children into Castle Park School in Dalkey, which at the time was an olde worlde West Brit type school: a throwback to an imaginary idyllic past.

A perfect example of Castle Park's unique charm was John Hurt giving a reading at the Christmas carol service that had everyone feeling they'd witnessed greatness. Every Christmas, on the last Friday before school broke up, the school put on a Christmas carol service. Although the school was predominantly Church of Ireland, they would invite the local Catholic priest for the service in St Patrick's Church, Dalkey. One special year John Hurt, whose son was in my daughter's class, read a passage from the Bible and it was quite thrilling for everyone. He probably could have read the whole Bible to us and everyone would have enjoyed it. Violet and I had come from a hard lonely British city existence to the soft connected suburban Dublin life. We met people through the local Church of Ireland or the school and we kept ourselves to ourselves. Family life was as good as it gets.

I was still working in the UK to maintain our lifestyle, travelling the length and breadth of the country. I'd fly or drive over on a Monday or a Tuesday and then back on a Friday while Violet got on with things in Ireland. I spent the weekends with my family while during the week I was living it up with the big job in the city. Mark and I would be out every night, up to all manner of activities my wife would not have approved of. These activities stopped short of adultery, but I was still doing far too much carousing.

Violet and I bought a house on an acre of land in Wicklow on the basis that we could afford it. Property prices around Dalkey were insane. Two examples: an ex-corporation terraced house in Dalkey was bought for 15k in the 1990s then sold in 2004 for 600k; a friend purchased a house in Blackrock – postage stamp garden, overlooking the shopping centre – paid €1.9 million. People from outside of Ireland were looking at us, thinking the Irish had lost their minds. Property was being bought with borrowed money and thus everybody forgot the true value of everything.

Buying multiple properties was one thing, but Violet and I had no such qualms when it came to spending our money. We had it to spend. With our children in the best local schools, we got involved in equestrian sports. I had never ridden before, but when Violet suggested it I jumped at the chance. Money was no object after all, so I kept telling myself.

The other riding club members thought we were *arriviste* millionaires and saw me as being overly flash. I was a little naive, but there is no lack of smugness in any riding club. The members watched with barely concealed glee as we hastily bought our first horse without any real idea of what we were doing. Instead of helping us make the right choice, they wanted to see us fail. Perhaps to a certain extent we deserved their scorn.

We got rid of that first horse very quickly, it was an ill thought out venture from the beginning. We waited, learnt more and bided our time until the right horse came along. This time Violet knew what she wanted and she bought a really good horse named Fido. Violet was much more talented than I was in the sport. She had Fido for ten years, a super horse, good at dressage, cross country and jumping; everything really.

Professionally, I had lofty ideas of transferring my UK success over to Ireland, with a view to eventually working in Ireland full time and spending more time at home with my family. Unfortunately, I have never quite come to terms with the Irish way of speaking and doing business out of both sides of their mouth. I recall my Dad telling me that the average Irish man would live in one ear and rent out the other at the same time.

Despite that, I believed I would be able to do some business in Ireland, especially when my UK client Tesco bought a large Irish supermarket chain . I was given an introduction to the manager in charge of mobiles. The manager in question assured me repeatedly,

"Yes we are definitely going to do business."

This was my introduction to paddy-whackery and codology.

Of course we never did any business. The long and the short of it, and there was far more long than short, was that this manager had no intention of switching mobile operator, our various business lunches were to serve some other purpose I was insufficiently Irish to grasp, lunch probably. In England I'd have been told "no the business is not up for grabs" and I would have moved on. The Irish way of doing business is completely different to anything I had ever experienced in the UK, it is much more between the jigs and the reels.

I also came across an infamous deal maker, well known in Ireland, who absorbed everything I knew about mobiles all the while dangling some business in front of me. It was a brain drain, my brain being drained into his; Paddy style. I should have learnt something about Ireland and its ways after I had wasted so much of my time messing around.

The whole experience brought to mind the rest of what my Dad told me prior to moving to Ireland.

"The Irish are not fools. Remember it pays to act the fool. That is the mistake the English have made for years. While the English are laughing at the thick Mick, the Irish are running rings around them."

In the end I gave up and decided to do all my business in the UK. Much as I loved living in Ireland and I truly did and do, I had no interest in doing business in Ireland. I could not handle the side mouth double speak way of doing business. I didn't really know what to make of it, so I happily went over and back to the UK every week, pretending I was not way over extended on my own accounts, living our idyllic family life in Brigadoon, followed by my salesman life, then followed by my rock and roll life.

What could possibly go wrong?

Chapter 13

LIVING IT LARGE

And so it went; I spent the week in London, nightclubs and strip clubs, the nineties salesman living large. I never did drugs, which is probably how I was able to sustain it for so long. Instead, I would quite regularly blow £1,000 a night in London on Champagne and strippers, which is equally as ridiculous. I suppose I could blame the decade, blame the nineties customer's demand for lap dancing and largesse, but I could have said no at any time and I didn't, I was content to lead my triple life.

At least I had Mark by my side. They really broke the mould when they made Mark Weir. One story gives a flavour of the type of shenanigans we were up to. Vodafone invited us to see Manchester United play Anderlecht in the Champions League in Belgium. We flew out on the team plane and got the coach to the hotel with the coaching staff and team. I sat next to Dwight Yorke and got a shirt signed by the whole team. We arrived into the team hotel and immediately Mark and I absconded around the town drinking. We came back in the early evening, fairly on it. I spent the first part of the evening chatting with some of the Man United coaching staff before I realised Mark was no longer with me, apparently he had absconded with a hooker.

I started chatting to a group of female American students who were travelling around Europe in style, staying in 5 star hotels. There were five girls amongst the group and I knew that Mark would not want to miss out. I hurried upstairs and got a hotel employee to let me into his room. He was lying on his bed stark naked and comatose, very *Pulp Fiction*. I shook him a couple of times to no avail, dead to the world. I whispered into his ear that there was a group of wealthy American students in their mid-twenties downstairs. Like Lazarus he leapt from the bed and within minutes he'd showered and we were back at the bar regaling the girls with our stories.

Coming up to midnight Mark and I announced we were going to a strip club, one of the American girls revealed she was bisexual and wanted to join us. Apparently she had never been to a strip club. So off we went. As soon as we got there I found myself alone ordering the Champagne, I was very wary of allowing the club to take my credit card to charge bottles of champagne to it. I knew the way these things went. When I went to pay for the second bottle I discovered we were being charged €500 a bottle. What a total rip off. Going off in search of Mark I finally found him getting a big kiss from a lap dancer while the American girl was giving the stripper a big kiss from below. Acrobats all of them.

"Mark, Mark we're being ripped off" I said, somewhat inconsiderately.

When he finally turned his face around to look at me through the sweaty fog of pleasure, I repeated myself.

"We are being ripped off."

Mark looked at me as if I had just told him the shipping forecast and replied slowly,

"Do I look like I care?"

To be fair, he didn't.

My weekends were on the exact opposite end of the spectrum, spent with the children, show jumping King my new horse and taking it easy. A far cry from the manic night-days in London. Violet and I were doing a lot of equestrian, perhaps too much. I was pretending to be a normal guy at the weekend. My marriage suffered as I was so worn out from the week that I was beginning to let things slip. There was no way I was putting in the work any marriage needs.

Then one day Anglo Communications was bought by Recall plc. Bingo, a big payday. Needless to say I blew it on cars and holidays. When Recall purchased Anglo Communications in March 2001 we had 5,000 subscribers and turnover was £225k per month. As of March 2002 Anglo was billing £1.1 million per month with 25k subscribers and the business was growing at a tremendous rate of 500%. Anglo were the fastest growing service provider in the UK Marketplace with the lowest churn[14]. We successfully developed business partnerships with Devon County Council, Rothschild's, Tibbett & Britten, Norbert Dentressangle, Clancy Construction, Mc Nicholas Construction, and BA.

Despite our business model being great we were heading for trouble. We were locked into a share purchase agreement. Recall had a deal with BAE Systems that sadly collapsed about 12 months after they bought us. Overnight our shares were worthless and we could not off load them. Suddenly we were sitting ducks, with a board of well-paid City directors and the company listed on the Alternative Investment Market.

Every month we were fighting to stay alive, we'd enough in invoices but we were not getting paid on time and it was killing us slowly. In one year everything Mark had built from scratch was destroyed on the back of one poor decision. We should never have sold to Recall but one of our investors had forced our hand and we were slightly blinded by the thought of a big payday. What if, what if, what if?

During this tumultuous period, Mark had been diagnosed with sleep apnoea; connected to stress. I began to suspect that the illness and the stress were clouding his judgement. He ultimately lost his way. I would like to think I was there for him as he would be for me later on. However it is mostly up to the person to find their way back and Mark would not be back for quite a while.

Mark and I relied on each other much more than we understood at the time; with Mark's illness our dynamic was diluted and rather than argue with him on some key decisions I may have acquiesced too easily. We were different people but we'd always complemented each other very well. I'd always been the more aggressive one, and whichever extreme either of us had veered to, the other would encourage them back to sense. This was no longer happening. The relationship and the business were unbalanced.

---

14 Customers changing to other providers

Anglo Communications went under because we were taken to the cleaners by two of our creditors. They played us like fools. One creditor in particular, 'John'; we met him in the Institute of Directors and he assured us he'd pay the £300k he owed Anglo. John and another creditor Dave, more of a common crook, realised we had liquidity issues. They used their knowledge of our predicament and the industry to manipulate the situation to their liking and our demise. John and Dave simply anticipated what we were going to do. They knew we were on borrowed time with a drum tight cash flow. Our solution to keep the business afloat was to factor the debt. We found a factoring company more than willing and they came in and financed us. They invoiced on our behalf and took a commission.

The £300k John owed us would have gone a long way towards steadying the ship. I wanted to shut him down but Mark wanted to give him the benefit of the doubt. We'd always seen the world differently and until then that had contributed to our success. John looked us in the eye and promised us he was going to pay and didn't. We lost the business. We discovered in the period in question that John and Dave had been re-invoicing and getting all their customers to pay them directly.

August 2002 the receiver arrived early one morning and announced himself. By coincidence, neither Mark nor I were there to meet him. And so ended Anglo Communications, the company faded away into oblivion.

From then on everything became a bit of a struggle for me. My life changed, I began to fall to earth, slowly at first. I was suddenly unemployed, with monthly outgoings of €10k. Mark had a break down and went AWOL. He met and married a Brazilian lap dancer and spent the next two years rediscovering himself and getting a lot of free lap dances. His life was never the same. Nor was mine. I still think a lot about those years, as I spent the next decade trying to get things back on track. Today I understand that my particular "track" was always leading me over the cliff. But I wasn't to learn that for a while yet.

Now looking back at that time, while I didn't have any affairs, I was not leading a healthy lifestyle for someone married and in their thirties. I'd blown a lot of money, and when Mark and I lost the business, I cursed myself for not having had the foresight to have put something away. I was right in the middle of my own debt disaster movie but I thought it was only a blip, a once off. Of course I thought the next thing was a once off as well, and after that it was a series of once offs. I'd spent the better part of five years living the Dalkey dream. It was now time to pay the consequences for my years in Brigadoon. The legend of Brigadoon is the story of a mythical village that emerges from the mist for one day every 100 years. This enchanted day is spent in joy and celebration. Those who happen up Brigadoon may remain in this beguiling place, only if they love another enough to leave the world outside. Dalkey was my Brigadoon.

Chapter 14

DESTROYING THE ILLUSION

Saying all that, I was not doubting my immortality yet. I was still manoeuvring around obstacles with a swagger. Surely, I thought to myself, all was not lost. I'd built up plenty of contacts over the years and I was confident I could get back in the game. I put myself out there once more, got a consultancy job in London and was hanging on to the vestiges of my equestrian set lifestyle. I jumped my horse King in the RDS in 2002. So while there was gloom around the corner, I did not recognise it yet. I presumed it was merely the shadows of my largesse.

In November of that year, I ill-advisedly went horse riding in Wicklow with a lot on my mind. King and I were following an inexperienced rider over a jump when her horse refused the jump, and turned sideways in front of the fence. I tried my best to pull King up, but the ground was very muddy and he lost his footing, stumbled and the two of us hit the ground. I ended up with a badly fractured femur – not an injury I would wish on anyone. Not to mention this was my second time breaking that same bone, albeit it on the other side. That day King knew I was in trouble , he stood over me as I lay on the ground with my very badly fractured leg. King knew an ill wind when he felt it. Who says horses are dumb animals? I can tell you King was not.

After being rushed into hospital and operated on the next day, I was incapacitated. The surgeon told me my nailed and pinned leg meant I'd be out for six months. I didn't have it in me to laugh but six months was a pipe dream, I had two weeks. I couldn't afford the luxury of lying in bed. I had to carry on. Once I could make it out of bed on crutches I went back to travelling back and forth to London. Driving was easier than flying – flying with the leg was an excruciating nightmare. Every time I squeezed into the micro space of economy class with my eyes closed, the head shaking regret coupled with life questioning pain made me swear never again. No fun.

Driving seemed the lesser of two evils, until winter January 2003, when I slipped on ice and broke the pin in my leg. Momentarily as I lay on my back after falling, as the pain shuddered into my psyche, withering me, I remember a warning briefly flashing through my mind. I ignored it. The fall set my recovery back a year.

How many signs did I continue to ignore? The fall had been my fault, nobody else had asked me to go out on that horse. I started to rely more and more on my mantras.

I have to take responsibility.

I have to keep the ship afloat.

I have to keep the show on the road.

I have to keep on limping forward.

My precious mantras, glib as they were, kept me going. Although my sense of responsibility has been a boon and a burden throughout my life, in those years it was often all I had as motivation. This slightly lunatic and intensely bizarre scenario carried on for a year.

Ireland had become very much home. But the commute was murder on my fractured aching bones and my disintegrating ego. I convinced Violet to move the family to the New Forest in Hampshire, England, close to where my offices were. By this stage I think we both understood things had gone amiss in our marriage, but it was one thing to understand it, quite another to do anything about it.

The children were not very happy about the move, but we all gave it a go. At this stage Ireland had been our home for 7 years but I believed there was opportunity in the UK for me, it was what I knew. I hoped there was a chance things would improve both in my professional and my personal life. I believed our closer proximity would help cure the separateness and the drift in our marriage, both had begun to take further toll. I knew I needed to spend more time at home, to stop being away all the time. Violet and I hoped moving to England would help repair the damage to our marriage. We were wrong. Our distance apart had allowed us to harbour the illusion that we still had a chance. Closer proximity was to destroy that illusion.

In the New Forest we replicated our Dublin lifestyle, put the horses in livery and continued competing in show jumping. I have never shaken the idea that our equestrian adventures had a lot to answer for: giving us both the opportunity to avoid each other whenever the other was free; giving us both a five year alibi to avoid the subject; and costing us an absolute fortune, 2k a month in livery fees alone.

We were in one of the most beautiful parts of England, wild ponies galloping around the New Forest. The people we met were extremely polite, nonetheless Fording Bridge did not feel like home. I missed the quirkiness of Ireland and my friends. Worst of all, my children were not happy. In August Violet and I came back to attend the Dublin Horse Show, and we both knew. But we had become experts in avoiding what was right in front of us.

The final straw came on a very low key New Year's Eve. Violet had gone to bed early and I looked around at the children and thought "this is not good." We all missed Ireland so much.

"Let's go home. Ireland is home." I said to myself as much as anyone else, but the whole house heard me and started packing immediately.

As for the marriage, Violet pretty much thought it was over. Maybe I did as well and didn't have the guts to say so, like a lot of men. I think my family might have resented me dragging them over to the UK. They probably did, but that is what families are for right? I'd felt that I could make it in the UK work wise, and I didn't. Ultimately the telecommunications industry had changed and I'd quickly become a dinosaur. There was not the same money to be made anymore. The trip had turned out to be a somewhat of a financial disaster and it left some deep scars on all of us. Despite everything, I feel it was an exercise worth doing because I learnt once and for all that Ireland was our home. Thankfully the children were happy to be back and that was great to see.

Violet and I continued to fade out of each other's lives. More than anything the respect had gone, from both quarters. We still loved each other, when you've loved someone that long it's almost impossible to ever fully lose the love, but we definitely needed our space. I went to live with a friend of mine, then got an apartment. After 4 months we decided to give it another go, to admit defeat was beyond either of us. This was the wrong decision and ultimately ruined the future for both of us. One of us should have had the courage to call it a day.

Coming back from the UK meant that I was back commuting.

I got involved in trading mobile minutes. I'd identified an opportunity and I was back trying to climb my way back to the top. Mobile minutes are traded on an exchange much like shares. This led me into more international circles and it was from there that I was to be given a chance to alter my self-inflicted circumstances and return us to the lifestyle we'd grown accustomed to. Whatever that meant and wherever the hell that was.

Chapter 15

AFGHANISTAN,
BACK ON TOP OF THE WORLD

I began trading minutes full time. As you would expect trading in minutes is primarily trying to find reliable value internationally. When the carrier business deregulated about twenty years ago, minute trading really expanded and there was a lot of money to be made in it. I was working in the UK selling international termination globally. Trading minutes is the stock exchange with minutes instead of shares; watching a screen, knowing the price, knowing what you can sell it for, what you can buy it for and of course making a margin. I was always pretty good at it.

My attention was repeatedly drawn to Afghanistan. After the US war with the Taliban, the market there was growing rapidly. I identified an opportunity and made contact with a company called Afghan Wireless. I met with the head of the carrier side of their business in London. He agreed that they might be interested in doing some business and invited me over to the US to meet with the CFO of Afghan Wireless's parent, Telephone Systems International. We got into a lengthy conversation on the GSM mobile business. Due to my background in the industry, I was able to give him some good advice on issues he was facing with Afghan Wireless.

"That's interesting. These things have been causing us problems for a long time." he told me.

No more was said. That night I went back to my hotel. The CFO emailed me and asked would I be able to meet again. I agreed. Now I was interested.

"Look you strike me as the type of guy that we could use. If you are interested we have a requirement in Afghanistan. We need someone to head up the sales department. Sales are not doing as well as they should be."

He offered me a job in Afghanistan.

In mulling over my decision, I thought about my disappearing marriage and the major financial pressure I was under. I desperately wanted my family to be able to continue to live the way they'd always done. The very idea of not being able to meet my requirements to my family struck real panic into me.

Afghanistan in the abstract represented, not an adventure or some danger lust fulfilment, but money. I rang Violet who might as well have been working for Afghan Wireless herself, she was so keen on the idea. She'd grown up in Northern Ireland and didn't see it as the risk others might have. She assured me with my military background I could look after myself. Initially I didn't bat an eyelid either, probably because of what I'd gone through in the army. It just didn't worry me. I don't mean to sound arrogant but that is the plain truth. And, deep down, the risk and the unusualness of it attracted me.

"This could get me back to where I need to be."

Another one of my mantras. My eternal search to get back to where I needed to be. Perhaps if I'd been more self-aware I might have realised this quest for the nirvana of where I needed to be was coming at a huge personal cost. But I wasn't. After being out injured I was back sprinting. Sprinting towards my new problems and away from my old, away from my merely personal issues towards some brand new altogether more serious type issues.

I believed I could make a difference, that I could be a success in Afghanistan. Although nothing I knew had prepared me for what I encountered; how could it? There was a natural apprehension, but I wasn't afraid. I had been close to drowning in debt since the business had gone under. I yearned to be away from worrying every minute of every day where the next chunk of cash was coming from. I knew I could take the burden and the pressure off Violet and my family. I also thought deep down that this might also help cure our marriage. It turned out I was right on some fronts and delusional on others.

In late 2005, Afghan Wireless made me an offer I couldn't refuse, so I duly accepted it.

I was to be based full time in Afghanistan. January 2006 I flew to Dubai and stayed there overnight. It was only then, floating on my back in a roof-top infinity pool with the Gulf filling the horizon, that I began to feel creeping tinges of anxiety.

"Shit! Tomorrow I am going to be in Afghanistan," occurred to me.

Momentarily as I floated I struggled to understand where I was or what I was doing. I gazed right back through my life, angry I'd made so many bad financial decisions, angry I was not sitting at home in Dublin living off a property portfolio. But there was no way back at that stage and the fear of my family losing everything far outweighed the fear I had of Afghanistan.

Nonetheless for the first time in my life, I felt truly scared.

Too late.

The next day I flew out of the old Terminal 2 in Dubai. Terminal 2 was used by airlines that could not afford to fly into Terminal 1. All the destinations on the board were straight from the headlines; places like Kabul, Kandahar, and Islamabad. I got on board the ramshackle Ariana Airlines, the Afghan carrier. It was falling apart literally. The plane was from the 1970s and a nervous traveller's worst nightmare. The plane filled unsurprisingly with Afghans and foreigners going to do business. The man beside me on the flight, going there to repair Humvees, asked me what I was doing going to Afghanistan. I told him about Afghan Wireless. He said that reminded him he needed to get a mobile sim when he arrived. My salesman mind immediately kicked in and I was already putting in place a deal to sell on flights.

Why don't we hand the sim cards out on the planes?

We had a lot of success doing our version of this in later months. We bribed the right people, always key, and sold the arriving passengers sim cards while they picked up their luggage in the Kabul terminal.

Kabul Airport was a shock. The war may have been over three years, but it looked like it was finishing the following week: burnt out planes at the side of the runway, craters everywhere you looked. The airport didn't have a baggage belt, it was total bedlam. Everywhere you looked there were bags strewn all over the floor. As soon as our bags were dumped, Afghans started running towards us shouting "baksheesh, baksheesh". I'd come from corporate England's tassels and loafers and the thought immediately occurred to me that I was not going to last five minutes in Kabul.

Eventually someone took my bag and ushered me out. I was not all there, I think I was vaguely in shock, vaguely in awe. When we got out the man carrying my bag was knocked out of the way by Wahid Khan an old Pakistani from HR holding a sign with my name on it. Wahid told me not to give the Afghan any baksheesh whatsoever. I gave him something anyway, what else was I supposed to do? Wahid shrugged and escorted me into a waiting car with three guards armed with automatic weapons inside. As well the guards in the car, there was a pick up in front with armed guards. I never went anywhere without this escort, you couldn't risk it.

Every guard had an AK47. Every building or structure, everything we passed was riddled with bullets, blood and dust. There was no left or right hand side to the road I could discern. Why would there be? Everybody had far more important things to be worried about, staying alive mainly. Traffic consisted of cars mingling, motor bikes weaving, donkeys moseying, and limbless beggars begging. It was the middle of winter in Kabul, meaning sub-zero temperatures. Any time we stopped, children would crowd around the window begging. One girl in particular reminded me of my youngest child, sitting that same day in a private school across the world. She was up begging at the window in her bare feet on her dirty tip toes. I handed her $10 despite Wahid urging me not to. He was probably right. Within a minute there were thirty more around the car, children only in their bodies, their dull adult eyes spoke of short perilous lives. I was startled and effected by this at first, but I soon got used to it, which says something melancholy and wise about me and Kabul I suppose.

We drove in our own little armed convoy to my accommodation on the outskirts of the town. The company owned accommodations called guest houses, with security guards on the door, barbed wire ringing the property. I met all the staff and the owner of the house, Mr Mana – a man I would come to know and respect: a friend whom I would never forget. Mr Mana ran the guest house. He was a very devout Muslim, an astonishing cook, as well as being probably the nicest person I've ever known. We used to call him Papa Smurf, because he was completely tiny and had a long goatee beard. Everyone who worked in Mr Mana's guest house was charming and I felt renewed hope.

Next I was brought to the office: a heavily fortified and guarded building. In the boardroom I was introduced to the CAO[15], Bassir Bayat, and my direct boss JMG, or Jean Michel. Jean Michel was an entitled Frenchman from central casting – arrogant, treated the locals like his servants, and displayed outright disdain for those around him. Jean Michel had an appalling way of dealing with people. I've been around plenty, but none as bad as him. Little did I or he know at the time, but the powers that be had already made up their minds; Jean Michel had to go. But I didn't know any of this at the time and I was pretty concerned at my poor welcome.

Jean Michel's hackles were up due to my arrival, they'd never been down his whole life. It was obvious from the outset he didn't want me there. He was right not to. However, I was still worried that they'd brought me all that way to work in a department headed by a guy who clearly wanted rid of me before I'd even unpacked. The other two in the office were Indian, Kaaliya and Tanish. I hadn't had much cause to work with Indians up until then. I was soon to learn that Indians from the north, and in Tanish's case Delhi, often held themselves aloof, they were the top of the caste ladder and they acted like it. Kaaliya could have been from anywhere, suffice to say he would have sold his own grandmother to anyone, an international sleazebag.

I'd been thrust into an environment with three people who wanted nothing to do with me. I would either sink or swim, or maybe die. It was an inauspicious start, but I really had nothing to lose. The first thing I noticed was Jean Michel never left the

15 Chief Administrative Officer

office, the consummate desk pilot. The two Indians definitely had no intention of ever leaving the office either; they said it was too dangerous. I was given the title of regional sales manager. I suspect Jean Michel *et al* regarded this as a poisoned Afghan chalice. I intended to do my job and go to the regions far away from them. I hoped my being out and about all over the country would bring into sharper focus Jean Michel's cowardly reluctance to leave the office.

At the end of my first day, I got back to the guest house and rang my family, and they all quizzed me on what it was like. I told Violet,

"You would not believe it. An Islamic Mad Max."

"Well you've got to do it, you've got to do it." The support I deserved.

Violet was worried I was going to come home. I'd never even told my mother where I was going. My time in Northern Ireland had taught me, where my mother was concerned, she presumed every death was automatically me until she had proof of life, or a phone call. I hadn't told my Dad either, owing in no small way to the lingering embarrassment at needing to do something so dangerous because of my own mistakes. It was difficult to hide or admit it when I spoke to my Old Man.

I spent a week in the office trying to work with Jean Michel, Kaaliya and Tanish. This mainly consisted of them stonewalling me on every request, constantly trying to make my life uncomfortable, their very own unsubtle version of constructive dismissal. I knew they were trying to get me to quit. I don't quit.

Chapter 16

THE OUTER REGIONS

I knew for certain I had to get away from the office and visit the regions, my regions. The six regional offices were Kandahar, Kunduz, Jalalabad, Mazar-e-Sharif, Herat and Khost. I went to meet Amin Ramin, head of security, a fearsome looking Afghan who glared at me, probably silently wondering what another bloody expat was doing in front of him. He would soon become a very good MD of the company, but to me he will always be Winston the Wolf from *Pulp Fiction*, the man who could fix anything. He was mister connected. His brother was the Minister for Agriculture and he knew everyone in Afghanistan. He was a ferocious looking, lethal individual, an ex-Mujahidin fighter who'd fought the Russians. He had a terrifying charisma. I liked him.

He spoke first before I had a chance to say anything,

"Great, another expat, here you come promising everything. But never delivering anything. Those three clowns downstairs, Jean Michel, Kaaliya and Tanish, they haven't delivered anything. What are you going to do different? What are you going to promise to deliver?"

Although I was slightly taken aback, I stood my ground.

"I don't know, I have to have a look around first."

Making clear he had heard it all before, he asked me,

"Yeah OK OK what do you need to do your job?" Presumably he was expecting to hear the usual drivel.

"I need two reliable guards and a suitable vehicle to go out and have a look at the situation in the regions."

I knew I needed to prove myself to management as quickly as possible. I'd surprised him I think.

"OK anything else?" he was still glaring but his demeanour had shifted a touch.

"I need my own weapon."

"No way you get a weapon. Are you crazy? What would you do with it?" Ideas of me driving the narrow and wide streets of Kabul drunk, taking pot-shots at imaginary foes no doubt. I explained to him I was ex-military that I'd been a weapons instructor as well as a trained soldier. He confided in me he was ex Mujahidin. I tried to be as blunt as I dared, and I explained politely but assertively,

"I am not driving round Afghanistan unarmed, end of story. I'm prepared to go out and do what needs to be done, but if I need to look after myself I'll feel a lot more comfortable with a weapon."

He thought about it for a minute looking at me, and agreed. I got a Glock as a sidearm and an AK47 for the regional travel, along with the necessary licence.

The following day, my new driver Rafiola, two guards and I left the office and began our tour of all the regional offices. I brought Engineer Abrar, who was to prove a great ally and wonderful friend. At all times we had pickups with armed guards escorting us. The only places we didn't go to by road over the next few months was Kandahar or Khost, simply because you couldn't, it was bandit country up by the Pakistan border. East Tyrone all over again, but less green and far more dangerous.

First we drove north to Mazar-e-Sharif: the fourth largest city in Afghanistan with a population of over 300k. It's the main city of its region and is known for its iconic blue mosques. In all the regional offices everybody was Afghan and most importantly from that particular region. In Afghanistan local knowledge is the only knowledge, it'll make you money and keep you alive.

When I arrived to the Mazar-e-Sharif office, I was not surprised to learn that nobody really knew what they were supposed to be doing. Sales personnel were making sales in a purely reactive way. They were merely order takers. The local Afghans wanted phones, so there was plenty of demand. Most of the staff in our offices had their job because of their relatives and friends. This is the way it is in Afghanistan. Over 80% of the population are Sunni with the remaining almost completely Shi'a. Irrespective, tribal loyalty and family loyalty rule the day generally.

In Mazar-e-Sharif, I met the regional manager and straight away he told me that no one had ever worked with him, no sales manager had ever visited from head office. Sales staff used to just sit there and do the best they could, mostly made up as they went along. All those highly paid expats sitting back in the fortified compound never going anywhere. Obviously, King Tut himself, Jean Michel, had never visited even once.

After Mazar-e-Sharif, I went to Kunduz – the fifth city of Afghanistan, the regional capital of the Kunduz province, and the main agricultural centre in the country. Kunduz is where they took the famous photograph of the ancient Kala-i-Jangi fortress crammed full of Taliban after they had surrendered to the Americans. The Americans were using it as a prison, and it was there that the CIA found John Walker, dubbed the American Taliban.

Incredibly, the regional manager of the Kunduz office was even more incapable than the first guy I'd met. It wasn't fair to judge them really. No one had ever trained them. Although all the regional manager ever did was come into his office, sit there and smoke cigarettes. I memorably met his cousin the marketing manager, who proudly said to me,

"Let me show you my marketing cupboard."

Whereupon he sauntered over to the marketing cupboard with me in tow and opened the door. I looked inside. It was full of absolutely everything: mugs, calendars, posters, and banners; all the marketing collateral going back years. Not one single item had ever been used. In his defence he thought he was doing a great job, he thought he was saving money.

I explained to him that all of it needed to be distributed and displayed. He looked distraught as he imagined his Aladdin's Cave being emptied. I asked him,

"What is the point of having ten thousand pens hidden away? They all need to be handed out to the schools and anywhere else that'll use them. Cups and mugs need to be handed out to all the coffee shops, the banners need to be up on the streets."

He was taken aback but he was listening, I continued,

"You're the best kept secret in Kunduz, nobody even knows you are here."

I spent a week working with the marketing manager talking him through the fundamentals. Of course I emptied his marketing cupboard, but he forgave me and was genuinely pleased in the end when he saw the difference the materials made. We had a good time working together. Overall I ended up spending a month in Kunduz. Together we took their monthly business from $200k to nearly $600k.

Head office noticed, and the Kunduz regional manager was named regional manager of the month. Within four weeks, he'd gone from being the least successful regional manager, to the most successful in Afghan Wireless. I educated the sales team, emphasising that instead of sitting in the office waiting for people to come to them, they needed to get out there and sell to the customers. We took every vehicle in our compound, packed them with staff and marketing material, and went out to surrounding villages and towns. The mobile phone is a vital part of the fabric of even the most rural Afghan village. They needed them and they wanted them. Mobile phones brought relatives and friends back into their lives that otherwise they may never have seen again, and also allowed the communication needed for trade.

We looked at towers and sites not generating any revenue and sold to the people in those areas. Straight away more people started connecting to our network. We gave the local traffic police fluorescent jackets with Afghan Wireless on them – free advertising for the company, increased brand awareness.

While I was in Kunduz, besides a bar and a German restaurant, there was nothing much else to do except work, so we worked. What sales angle did we have? Well truthfully we didn't really need one. Afghans wanted mobiles and often they'd never been actively sold to before. So they were delighted. Many tended to be illiterate. We used the local dealers, who had a better handle on the sales landscape. The sales team had never been shown how to go out there and sell. I demonstrated to them that I was prepared to leave the office to go out and sell.

And like anywhere on earth, leading by example remains the most effective management technique.

I have always endeavoured to avoid being the aloof expat expert that lived to order the locals around. Besides the fact that I got on with the Afghans easily, I've never believed I've some God given right to be respected. I believe respect needs to be earned. It's not something you should expect, it's something the person should give freely. This would range from eating my food with my colleagues and sharing bread with them, to working alongside the team. I proved I was prepared to be proactive and get out there, to work and sell. I never asked anyone to do anything I was not willing to do myself. I was another part of the team. We travelled around all the villages together, anywhere they went I went, unless I thought it was too dangerous and then nobody went. Straight away the sales teams saw I meant business and responded well. If he's doing it, why shouldn't we.

When I returned to Kabul my arch enemy Jean Michel tried to orchestrate my ousting. He stormed into my office, convulsed with some trumped up charge, determined to antagonise and provoke me into leaving.

He told me,

"You're completely disruptive, you're not a team player." And then absurdly,

"I only told you to go and visit the regions for a week, and you stayed for four weeks."

I responded,

"You never told me anything whatsoever, you never told me to go anywhere as you wouldn't speak to me. I'm not sure you said a single word to me in the whole week before I went."

A scene that perfectly encapsulates the overly macho world of expat intimidation and posturing.

Jean Michel then resorted to abusive mails, I warned him that abuse and rudeness would not be responded to either. I felt more self-assured after I had proven myself, therefore I was prepared to make a stand. Physically he could not intimidate me, which made him angry, and in his anger his treatment of everyone around him deteriorated further. Rather than dwell on his outrageous behaviour, I will say that he was the one who got ousted. However, I was in the dark about this when I was summoned to America. They flew me to the States, over to our parent company, I was nervous. Immediately I was told,

"Those three guys don't want you there."

Outwardly I remained calm.

"OK"

"We are going to get rid of them." I exhaled with relief.

"Really, we couldn't let you go. Unlike a lot of guys we've come across, you actually do what is written on the tin, you talk big but you deliver big as well. So we'd like to make you sales and marketing director. I suggest you keep Tanish, what you do with Kaaliya is your choice, but Jean Michel is gone."

The word 'payback' loomed large in my mind crossing the globe back to Afghanistan. Jean Michel had always treated everyone around him appallingly, but in particular his driver seemed to suffer his whims. Jean Michel made the man stay in his car all day in the freezing cold for no reason. Worse while out in the freezing Afghan nights, he'd insist the driver waited in the car while he spent three, sometimes four hours in a restaurant, again for no discernible reason other than power lust.

I was allocated Jean Michel's vehicle, but I kept Rafiola and relocated his driver. I also refused him the use of it as a form of petty revenge. Very unlike me, I am not a spiteful person, but I wanted him to get a taste of his own medicine, not really for my benefit but for the benefit of the employees. I made sure that for his final trip out of Kabul, Jean Michel got Farid's car: the worst car in the fleet.

Farid drove a battered old Toyota Corolla, it was in appalling condition and was used to transport crap, much like Jean Michel. It did not even have the right security passes to enter the airport. This meant he had to walk the last mile to the airport all on his own with his bags, scuffing along tail between his legs, and without his bonus. The transport manager who'd suffered Jean Michel's wrath more than most, had the pleasure of telling Jean Michel he would be traveling in Farid's Corolla. The servants, his staff and I were all delighted to see the guy go.

One story in particular encapsulates Jean Michel's approach to the people around him. After one of his shirts was ruined in the laundry, he made a big song and dance about it. Eventually he bullied one of the men working in the guest house into admitting it was his fault. Jean Michel made him pay $50 to replace the shirt. The man would have been on $200 a month or less, but to Jean Michel it was always about his ego and his desire for dominance.

Nobody whatsoever bid him farewell.

Not a single person in all of Afghanistan was sorry to see him go.

So ended my first day as head of sales for Afghan Wireless.

My Parents 1963

Christmas 1967 with my Father

Dublin 1980 in my Grove disco days

Grandfather John Barry

Great Grandfather Patrick Nolan

South Tyrone 1980s front row kneeling

South Tyrone 1980s

In my ceremonial dress uniform

Windsor Castle Guard 1985

Charging down the Bayonet assault course as a recruit

Typical 1980s riot scene
Photographer Sean Hillen

Sales man of the nineties

Cavan Equestrian Centre 2002 with King in a jump off final

With my dear friend engineer Abra

If looks could kill, Afghanistan 2006

Chapter 17
LOCAL POLITICS

I slotted into the sales and marketing job, determined to make the most of it. I continued to travel around the country meeting all the regional managers, assessing the situation and helping; I was determined to be a success.

Kabul was full of ex-military mainly working for security companies and NGOs. The security at the embassies was primarily outsourced to ex UK, US and South African military. I got on OK with the security people, being ex-military myself.

Afghanistan adheres to the Arabic weekend, Friday and Saturday. I tended to work the Friday anyway but I liked to have Saturday off. I would visit a souk or one of the shopping malls. There were certainly bars to go to, but the best places in Kabul were Chinese brothel-restaurants. Everywhere you looked there were Chinese restaurants doubling as brothels. The waitresses served food and also worked as prostitutes on the side, or maybe it was the other way around? You could get a very nice meal of an extremely high standard, then entertain yourself with a waitress. When I went there I never involved myself with the ladies, but I did enjoy the singular atmosphere. Curiously, living in a semi war zone can often be a dull affair, and we all needed to unwind from the relentless tension.

Our favourite was called the Happy Hour Café. The Mama San, Wen Wen, was a tough cookie who supported her whole family back in China. She played the worst music I've ever heard, bar none. It was frightening. She allowed me on occasion to play my iPod for a little aural relief, but in general it was a tortured cacophony of various countries' greatest hits. You could get hashish in the Happy Hour Cafe, put it on the shisha, and get off your head. There was gambling, hookers, drugs and booze, a spicy Kabul melange.

The Happy Hour Café bar was like the bar from Star Wars, a monsters' ball of security contractors, soldiers, expat wannabees and various other nationalities and ethnicities from all over the solar system. It's a wonder there was not more trouble there, as it was Afghanistan and in Afghanistan everyone is armed. The only time I was ever involved in any type of physical altercation, was when one of a group of ex Indian Army Ghurkhas, working as private contractors, started slapping around a Chinese waitresses. I was having a drink with a six foot four American friend at the time and I leaned over and said to the ex-Ghurkha,

"Very easy to slap a woman around. Not so easy to slap a man around. Why don't you have a go at me?" I am not really sure what I was thinking speaking to a Ghurkha like that. But I said it with the help of about 8 large glasses of Johnny Walker Black Label.

The Ghurkha came at me, threw a punch, I threw a punch. Briefly it kicked off as everyone got involved in the melee. It was a soldier's fight, no weapons. A mass brawl in the middle of a Chinese brothel. Although there were guns everywhere, not one shot was fired and not one gun was drawn. It was broken up by the arrival of the ex-Ghurkhas' commander. The officer walked up to the original offending Ghurkha and crowned him with a lead lined baton. After being reprimanded by his officer, he came over to me to apologise. While he was apologising a different Chinese waitress smashed a bottle over his head from behind, he did not flinch.

The vivid red blood trickled down his face as he finished apologising. Expressionless he turned to her, looked straight through her, turned back to me, wiped the blood off his forehead, shook my hand and left.

That was a rare occurrence. The x-factor involved, of never quite knowing who you were getting involved with, the smoking, the danger all around, meant that places like the Happy Hour Café were relative oases in the midst of the encroaching danger.

In Afghanistan family is everything, there was no point in us fighting a national culture that has existed for millennia. When it comes to giving out jobs, Afghans give them to their families, without exception. My job was then to cajole, train, explain and in very extreme examples transfer our Afghan employees. I enjoyed this aspect of the job immensely.

Of the two Indians in my department, I kept Tanish who, despite being a pompous ass, was an excellent marketer. He simply had that Delhi way about him, for want of a better description. But he knew his stuff, he understood the need for a coherent marketing strategy and was good at coming up with campaigns. I was learning on the job. I'd never done any marketing, I learnt a good deal from him. We ended up developing a good working relationship once Jean Michel had been eliminated. Tanish eventually left us to work in Africa.

Kaaliya was a different matter. I couldn't decide if I wanted to keep him or let him go. I told him that he was on a three month trial, and that he would have to change how he operated if he wanted to stay. He had this subservient cap doffing routine, constantly offering to carry my briefcase, opening doors for me, it used to drive me up the walls. Subservient bullshit. Jean Michel had obviously loved all this, but it went against what I wanted to instil. I was forming a results driven team. Kaaliya was an unusual man, but I still wanted to keep him on. I really hated admitting defeat and firing people. However it was all brought to a head one day when he damaged his own laptop, was seen doing it, then blamed it on someone else because he wanted to get them fired. Luckily some of the house servants witnessed the incident and I fired Kaaliya on the spot.

I hired a Pakistani, Awais, from Karachi as my new sales manager. In general, I found Pakistanis very good to work with. All very honourable, stuck to their word. Awais went out and travelled the country meeting people and putting together sales campaigns. The team responded well to him and he was generally successful.

The Afghan Wireless business structure was such that each city had an exact replica of the head office. We always hired the regional manager from the area, they were able to navigate local politics, and had the contacts needed to make things happen. There was absolutely no point in putting an expat of whatever ilk in charge at a local level, zero. Our ability to train our employees was at the heart of the success we enjoyed. Dealing with individuals you realised what was needed. So what if the marketing manager was a cousin not a marketer, no matter, we worked with them and trained them as marketers and sure enough almost always we'd have success.

In 12 months we increased AWCC's turnover from $4 million to $10 million.

We were increasing revenue and sales month on month. Central to this was an exclusive deal I'd secured with Ashraf from Peshawar. Ashraf's family had been traders for centuries, they had continued trading during the Taliban times, were part of the intricate tapestry of the country, and gave us access to markets we'd never have known about. Ashraf traded all over Afghanistan.

He'd often come sit in my office and we'd talk about family and friends, share our varied stories: chew the fat. Our primary business consisted of selling top up cards and Ashraf treated them as a commodity, much like the Nestle milk powder he also traded in. This proved to be a very lucrative sales channel and ensured that everywhere Ashraf traded sold our sim cards and our top up cards. We gave him an 8% discount for bulk orders, and he would keep 3% and pass on the other five to the outlets. Ashraf was dealing in millions of $USD, so 3% was a nice margin to have.

Sadly Ashraf was assassinated in November 2008. He was sitting in his car on a normal lethal Afghan afternoon, shot dead and no money was taken. I was very saddened to hear it, as I'd always liked him. People suggested it was something to do with a financial dispute, although knowing him as I did, it was over someone owing him money rather than the other way around. No one really knows why, but it stopped me in my tracks when I heard about it. All I could picture was his face and the expression he'd always use when he wanted something from me,

"What to do Mr Alan, what to do?"

Another person I'll never see again. On earth anyway.

My relationship with Amin Ramin had improved, and with him as the MD we turned the company around. I ran everything past him first, always made sure I had his support before I embarked on any new plans. This was essential, I needed his opinions and insights into the complexities of the political and business landscape of Afghanistan before implementing any strategies.

Anywhere I have worked before or since I have always sought the loyalty of the local staff. In Afghanistan my staff had my back and I had theirs, they kept me informed of what was going on around me and I made sure to be in their corner if they needed me. I ran my department along loose military lines. Everyone understood that we worked as a team and we did things for each other.

When you look at Islam, a subject never out of the news, like most anything there is a good side and a bad side to it. All we ever see in the West is the bad side: Jihad, suicide bombers, people flying planes into buildings, blowing up buses, ISIS killing people simply because they are not of the same faith or not the right type of Muslim. But my own experience of Islam when I lived in Afghanistan and Iraq was quite different. The people I encountered there were some of the most decent human beings I've ever met. An Afghan who earned $200 a month would not hesitate to give you the shirt off his back. If you walk into a room in Kabul and there are two Afghans sitting eating Afghan bread and that is the only food they have in the world, they offer you a third of their bread every time. I have met so many decent Muslims that it has made me ashamed at how our Western media portray them.

Every now and again, we would have a barbeque out the back of the guest house. We could just about see the minarets of the mosque next door. There were some Germans in the house along with me and we could get as much pork as we wanted from the UN shop. For the most part, Mr Mana would insist on barbequing for us. But we never asked him to cook pork. I asked him once what would they do next door in the Mosque if they ever smelt the pork. He didn't seem overly worried. He told me that most Afghans have no idea what pork smells like so it was not an issue, we both laughed. During Ramadan we would be happy to respect our hosts by not cooking pork, as a mark of respect for the Muslim's holy month.

Mr Mana could make soup better than any chef I've ever come across. I was always on at him to open up his own line to sell in Harrods. As a bit of fun, I asked the graphics guy in marketing to design a label, "Mr Mana's Soups of Kabul". We all had a laugh and he really enjoyed the compliment. By the time I left, he was doing soup for all the surrounding guest houses. Whenever we both had a free evening we'd wile it away happy and melancholy in the garden, talking slowly and quickly about our lives and our families, sipping Afghan Cha. Two humans.

The mosque next door had three different mullahs performing the five daily calls to prayer, one castrated, one cranky, one harmonious. Crazy Ed with a PhD in rocket science had been living with us in the guesthouse for a couple of months. He was an American. While socially inept Crazy Ed had some problems fitting in with us Europeans, he really couldn't fathom the Afghans. In particular he seemed to have a little Jihad of his own going against Islam. Each month he became more and more disturbed, each month he would spend more and more time in his room rocking back and forth on his rocker until he pretty much fell off it. It came to a head during a final call to prayer of the day. I heard him at his window screaming at the top of his lungs at the voice coming from the minaret on the mosque,

"Shut up, shut up."

"Shut up, shut up."

Head stretched out, neck craning at the sky, wailing at the Islamic prayers he so hated.

"Shut up, shut up."

"Shut up, shut up."

This was not the first time he'd been disrespectful with the locals, but it was the worst. I ran into his room and grabbed him back inside, much to his dismay. We had him transferred home before he got himself and us all killed.

Poor Crazy Ed, ranting about his beloved bacon, and shouting at the real and imaginary voices in his head. He was a staunch Republican who apparently had an IQ off the Richter Scale. He thought he knew everything, although he'd only been in telecoms for a couple of years. Ed kept telling us about his blessed PhD in rocket science. He was highly intelligent but socially apart, and there was a real sense of relief around the guesthouse when he went home.

My remit had evolved during my time in Kabul and I found myself travelling all over the region, particularly India, recruiting and interviewing staff. It was there that I met my first Anglo Indian. An Anglo Indian is a white-skinned, blue-eyed Indian. This man was called Kevin O'Keefe. My guide brought him over as he looked like an Irish guy but sure enough he was Indian. I was charmed by his name and easy manner. Kevin worked in an Indian restaurant in a place called Nasik in the middle of nowhere, very far off the beaten track. His Irish great grandfather had come to India to build the railways and stayed on. Later my guide explained that for Kevin being white meant he was often discriminated against inside their strange caste system. Yet another experience I would never have had if I had not taken up the expat lifestyle.

I've always tried to help the locals when I could, wherever I was and whoever they were. In Afghanistan when I was asked I'd help out with various unexpected expenses. This tended to be in the form of some cash for family matters. In the beginning I helped people I knew, Afghans who worked in the guest house and Rafiola. Eventually as word got around I had to ask Mr Mana to have a word with those who didn't work in the guesthouse, tell them to stay away. Unfortunately it had gotten out of hand. I would get home after work to a few Afghans waiting in the hall for a private consultation. It was like a doctor's surgery. My multinational colleagues were complaining, telling me I was considered a soft touch and that as a result they were being pestered as well.

Afghanistan is no place for the faint hearted, but I have to say I wanted to help, soft touch or not. This was not about loaning a fiver to a friend in the boozer, the people asking were not squirrelling money away, they truly needed it. The Afghan custom is to ask those more fortunate for help in times of trouble. OK maybe I never learnt my lesson, but perhaps it was a lesson I was reluctant to learn.

My expat colleagues always arrived at work en masse at eight o clock every morning. I was wired up about IEDs[16] and ambushes from the moment I arrived in Kabul. I hadn't forgotten the dangers of creating a pattern that could be turned into intel, intel that attackers could then use.

On one particular day, I'd arrived early into the empty parking lot and was walking across the road to the office when I spotted a woman sitting with a child, no more than three years of age. The child's arm had been severed at the wrist, the arm so badly burned I could barely stand to look at it, the woman was in tears. I couldn't walk past her, nor believe the anguish in her eyes. It was a horrific sight that appalled me. I'd been told numerous times not to give money to the Afghan beggars. I handed her a $100 bill and was about to tell Rafiola to bring her to the hospital when all the guards game running over. One grabbed her, another grabbed the child's charred severed limb and yanked it, I recoiled horrified. Above the woman's protestations the guard showed me an animal's limb, definitely not a child's, the bone had been stuffed up the child's sleeve. The child seemed drugged and supine.

I asked Rafiola,

"What the hell is going on here?"

"She's a professional beggar, you shouldn't have given her any money, look look." Rafiola said, as the guard continued to wave the bone, the fake child's arm. They took the money off the woman and gave it back to me. I didn't really know what to think, I was not happy. What kind of life was this woman and her poor kid living, a type of grotesque begging show, it was awful. The guards and Rafiola looked at me like I was a mug. For a while that incident gave me the harsh callous shell necessary to prevent me from acknowledging any of the grief stricken stories I witnessed every day.

16 IED Improvised Explosive Device.

Yes, it hardened me for a while, until we were in Jalalabad a few months later. Engineer Mohammed, Abrar and myself were visiting dealers, weaving in and out of the market stalls. I spotted a very young, horribly disfigured crippled child using two pieces of wood to propel himself along in the dust, well maybe more dragging himself along the filthy dirty ground, no more than ten years of age. I have to say, despite everything I'd already seen, I was shocked. I had to do something about it.

I have no idea why I thought I always had to be the expat saviour, but I am a glutton for punishment. I spoke to Engineer Mohammed and asked him whether we could get the boy a wheelchair. I was to be in Jalalabad for a week. I told the child to be at our office that afternoon. The wheelchair cost me $200 and when the child turned up at the office, I gave him the wheel chair and a hundred dollars and wished him the best, I felt good knowing the boy would not be crawling around in the dirt anymore and I walked around a little lighter the next couple of days.

Two or three days later, we were back in the market and of course the child was back dragging himself through the dirt begging.

"Where's the wheelchair" I asked in exasperation to no one in particular.

Engineer Mohammed answered me, "His father sold the wheelchair because it would affect his begging."

That's when you get a wakeup call. You can do these good deeds and you can try to help. But you really need to be channeled in how you do it. Unfortunately the harshness of the land is more easily changed through slow seismic shifts. Did I learn my lesson that day? I have no real idea what the lesson was supposed to be. Don't give beggars money? Do give them money? To this day I don't really have a firm grip on what I was supposed to have done and I don't begrudge any of them what they got. Professional beggars or not, I wouldn't do it, and they are welcome to whatever they can get. It's a godawful tough life they lead.

Chapter 18

THREE FLIGHTS CLOSER

The first dusty year in Afghanistan went by very quickly, I was back in Ireland every three months for at least a week. I also had quite a few meetings in Dubai, so I was in and out of Kabul and the UAE quite often. Each time was an emotional roller coaster. Four flights stand out as I got closer and closer to death.

Dubai Kabul Ariana Airlines.
A few minutes after we took off from the Dubai tarmac, all the passengers were still trying to sense whether the plane had enough oomph to get up. The plane levelled off and started to fly in tight banked circles over the Arabian Gulf. The captain came on the loudspeaker and said something in Pashtun. Suddenly the cabin crew looked very worried. When I asked what was going on, the ashen faced crew replied that we were dumping fuel. Ariana Air was a bankrupt airline, so it had to be something serious for the plane to be dumping fuel. We eventually turned back and landed in Dubai. By this stage everyone was borderline petrified. When the plane came back in to land, it landed like a MiG screeching to a halt. We were all quickly evacuated. It turned out the hydraulics had been leaking.

When I finally got back to Kabul my friend played me the TV news clip of my plane landing in Dubai with smoke coming out of the back of it. Afterwards they had to close the runway for other flights while they towed our plane off. Funny thinking of that heap of junk blocking all those shiny new Emirates aircraft from landing. It was a lucky escape but no big deal.

Dubai Kabul CamAir
A Finnish friend and I were flying over Afghanistan towards Kabul, when the pilot came on the loudspeaker and in an American accent announced that we were going to have an in-flight quiz. We were all given paper and pen to write down our answers. The American pilot started asking random quiz questions.

Next thing,

"For those of you who have not seen Kandahar it is to the right of the plane",

He proceeded to tip the plane to the right to afford us a better view. By this stage, what with the tipping and the quizzing, everyone was beginning to wonder whether the pilot was doing enough piloting.

Kabul is 4,000 feet above sea level, surrounded by some of the highest mountains in the world, both of these factors give it an extremely unique flight path in and out from any direction. On our approach to Kabul Airport, our quiz master decided to bring us in his own way. Immediately it felt all wrong and I became extremely anxious. Next thing the engines roared as he abandoned his landing and we were flying right between the mountains. Out the window we could see bewildered villagers looking up at us in terror from no more than thirty or forty feet away. I thought, "Right, we're dead." This was not long after another plane from the same airline had flown into the same mountain in identical circumstances. Everyone on the plane started praying and crying, myself included.

That particular flight was probably the most frightened I had ever been in my life. Until my next flight.

The final flight Kabul Delhi Air India.

Immediately after we took off from Kabul, we started banking severely. There was a loud thud and the plane levelled off at around two thousand feet – nowhere near high enough to get over the surrounding mountains. This pilot was a genius as he guided us in and out between peaks. Unable to fly the plane above them, he had no other choice. We could see the mountains vividly from no more than twenty feet. All the passengers were too scared to even breathe, everybody concentrating on not disturbing the pilot. The only time I have ever experienced a flight like that was in the cinema. He got us down. When we disembarked the aircraft, on the left hand side we saw the engine had picked up debris on take-off and this had caused it to explode. I laughed. What else was I going to do? Cry?

Chapter 19

WHO WANTS TO BE AN AFGHAN MILLIONAIRE?

After two years with the company, I became chief commercial officer, with a sales director and a marketing director both reporting into me. With my knowledge of the industry I was given a lot of responsibility. I had a very good working relationship with my boss in the States, Dan. He worked for Telephone Systems International (TSI), our parent company.

We were approached by Abdullah who claimed to have the Afghanistan rights for the highly successful TV show *Who Wants to be a Millionaire*. We were very interested and I entered into negotiations with him but nothing was happening: echoes of my Irish adventures. I got the impression after three months or so that he was talking rubbish, he was spoofing. I did a bit of research, and found out that the rights for *Who Wants to be a Millionaire* were owned by Sony Media. I contacted the actual person in charge, who said,

"Yes I am aware of the gentleman in Afghanistan, Abdullah, but he has not paid the required deposit."

I wasn't sure what he meant, I asked him,

"What do you mean by deposit?"

"Well for us to enter into exclusivity you would need to pay us ten thousand dollars. And then we'll give you the exclusive rights to *Who Wants to be a Millionaire* in Afghanistan. We have asked Abdullah on several occasion but he hasn't paid the money."

It was becoming obvious to me that unfortunately my friend Abdullah was at best a chancer, a wannabe deal maker with no capital behind him. Why did I need Abdullah in the first place? From then on I dealt directly with Sony Media. We signed the non-disclosure with them, and entered into an agreement granting us exclusive rights to the programme in Afghanistan. This was the all clear to go ahead and produce the programme in partnership with Ariana TV; our sister company. We devised a programme schedule, we paid for the set, which was flown in already built and ready to put together. Initially we had been thinking about filming in India as opposed to Kabul, because it was thought that Kabul wouldn't have the facilities. But common sense prevailed and we found the studio space we needed.

We hired famous Afghan TV presenters and made sure to have an all Afghan studio audience. It was a very good way of generating revenue, all the communications were exclusively through the Afghan Wireless network. If you wanted to appear on the programme, you had to send a text message using Afghan Wireless. The entrance questions were generated through Afghan Wireless, answering the questions correctly was the only way to qualify as a contestant on the show. It was a real coup for Ariana TV, for Afghan Wireless and for me personally. The broadcasts were reported around the world as a sign of Afghanistan opening up again. Internationally, female contestants in particular were seen to be a positive development for the country.

Jokingly one day I suggested to Bassir, the owner's brother, that he might be interested in doing an Afghan version of *The Apprentice*. Bassir was always firing people; his day was not complete unless he had ruined someone else's. I mentioned it to him,

"Why don't we do an Afghan *Apprentice*? You already fire people every day in work, this would be another way to make that pay. Every week we could have you telling someone "you're fired" live on national TV."

The joke was short lived as Bassir, never known for being the wit of the group, thought I was being serious and had already begun to envision what he was going to wear. I had to tell him I'd only been joking. He did not take too kindly to it; so that was the end of that.

Naturally as a result of being away all the time, what was left of my marriage fell further asunder. And while financially we were back on top, whenever I came home I felt Violet regarded me as an inconvenience. She had her life and my coming home for a couple of weeks did not fit into that life. As soon as I arrived she was waiting for me to leave. But my children were in Ireland and I loved to spend time with them.

When back in Dublin, I slept in the spare bedroom. But at least I was unarmed. That was something.

Chapter 20

THE RETURN OF THE NEVER GONE AWAY TALIBAN

By 2008 I had a department of 200 people with six managers reporting directly to me. However, I no longer felt secure in the guest house, the security was slipping. More and more I'd come home to find the guard asleep with his weapon out of reach: an easy target for any attackers. The guards were almost pointless anyway. It began to prey on my mind. Especially the idea of a kidnapping, I felt uncomfortable relying on other people for my security. My bedroom balcony offered a means of escape and I spent some time working through what I would do if they came for us. No point in planning your exit while they are kicking in your door, preparation is always best. I was not going to wait in my room if I heard a commotion downstairs. I was going to get out of there. I slept in a locked room with a chair under the door handle, a Glock on the bedside table. Kabul had become an extremely dangerous place all over again and I was worried.

When I first arrived in Kabul, it was relatively safe and I tended not to even carry my side arm most of the time. As the years went by, in contrast, Kabul began to tighten, the air crackled and once more no one and everyone was everywhere. There was an increase in the number of suicide bombings and people were talking about how the Taliban were back and had infiltrated the Afghan Police and the Afghan Army. I flew the Irish flag from our back garden, I was not sure it would do any good but it might give someone pause and it made me feel slightly more secure.

Many of the bars closed down and all the Chinese brothel restaurants went in a mass clean up by the Afghan Police. There were even more suicide bombings.

An American truck, five or ten ton crashed into five cars because its brakes failed. Or as others claimed the Americans' SOP, their standard operating procedure, was to drive as fast as possible through the cities. After, when the crowd got angry, the

Americans or the Afghan National Police or whomever opened fire into the crowd with a 50 calibre machine gun, killing more people. The crazed convoy then drove over another car on their way out.

There was a criminal element to the outraged crowd, as criminals realised the rampage was an opportunity to loot. The mob ended up outside our office trying to smash the door down. We could see them surrounding the building on the CCTV. I grabbed my AK47 and went around the back. We were on the third floor, and the only way into the building was up the large central staircase. I knew I'd be able to get out through the boardroom on to the roof. I thought if I see anyone come in the doors I'll give them the good news. I was not prepared to be captured. No way was I being taken hostage.

Thankfully it died down later that day. The doors held and although every single vehicle in the transport department was burnt out and the security hut was destroyed, we were all OK. They also tried to get into the Aryana TV building and that ended up like the siege of the Alamo. At one stage, the Ariana presenters were appealing live on TV to the Interior Minister to rescue them. In the end the rioters found a new target. They destroyed the offices of an aid company. The wisdom of mobs.

It was highly unlikely that we were going to be taken hostage, as I suspect it was not insurgent led. But we would surely have been killed, as the mob's anger was raw and fuelled by more than the one incident. It was a wonder there were not more crazed mobs. Worst of all, they also burned down a pizzeria in that well known mob fervour, visible worldwide, of destroying anything that symbolises difference or foreignness. There was a curfew that day.

I missed those pizzas.

Everybody in Kabul knew the Taliban were back and had infiltrated the Afghan security forces: the police and the army. After their initial defeat, the Taliban had retreated back into the mountains and into Pakistan. As the years passed they trickled back. One day in Kabul there were two suicide bombings that acquired their intended targets. I stupidly asked the head of security was it safe to leave the building and he looked at me as if I was a lunatic and said,

"You tell me. Nowhere is safe today." He shook his head.

That day I left the building with my Glock and sat in the front seat, put the guard in the back making sure he understood my own SOP: that if anyone remotely resembled someone who might detonate a suicide bomb they were to be shot between the eyes. I got home without incident.

Another murderous Kabul afternoon, Rafiola and I were driving up to our Jalalabad Road office. The road was known as Dodgeville due to the number of military compounds up there; it also was an extremely wide road, so all in all it was lethal. Firstly we heard an almighty explosion, in the distance I saw debris flying in the air. It was a UN convoy caught by an IED bomb blast. The explosion went on for an eternity within those split seconds, we turned around and decided not to visit the office that day. It could wait. Another daily stark reminder of where we were. The real value was that it served as a clear example for Rafiola as to why we should never follow convoys too closely, something I had been at pains to explain to him. I wanted him to understand that IEDs don't care, they kill everyone and foreign convoys were the most prized targets out there.

Kandahar, the second largest city in Afghanistan is very hot, very dusty, rammed full of Taliban and the feeling that it could kick off at any moment. A most worrying place. As tensions built country-wide, I was in Kandahar when the Taliban attacked the prison, killing nine police officers and eight prisoners: a devastating attack resulting in all the other prisoners escaping. The attack consisted of a suicide truck bomb at the front gate, a suicide bomber at the back gate and rockets fired by Taliban riding motor cycles. 600 prisoners escaped in total. No messing. These type of incidents were daily occurrences and we just got used to them. That was the way of life in Afghanistan.

In 2008, an Italian consultant and I had to go to Jalalabad near the border with Pakistan by helicopter. The head of security walked up to me as we were getting on board and handed me an extra magazine for my AK47 and another clip for the Glock. The Italian looked aghast and asked,

"What do you need that for? We're going by helicopter?"

I replied,

"Well almost all of the territory we are flying over is under Taliban control. Granted it is highly unlikely we would survive if we got shot down so there is probably nothing to worry about. But if we have to make a forced landing and we survive, we'll need some protection while we wait for help. And this is our protection. Two magazines, 60 rounds of 7.62 mil and the Glock's two 15 rounds of 9 mil. If we have to use the 9 mil then they are very close and we are in deep shit. So I will save the last two for you and me."

I laughed, he didn't. He looked a touch green, as well he might. I was not mocking him. I was deadly serious. That part of the world had laid waste to larger forces than my Italian colleague and I. 160 years before on the road to Jalalabad, the Afghans had wiped out a retreating British garrison.

The beginning of the end came on 6th January 1842, when the garrison left Kabul and fled towards Jalalabad to return to the comparative safety of India. The garrison contained British and Indian soldiers, 4,500 soldiers, including 690 Europeans and British civilians, 12,000 wives, children and civilian servants.

The journey was hell. From the moment they left Kabul they came under sustained attack. This was despite having left British officers and their families along with most of their guns as hostage to ensure safe passage. Every night saw civilians and soldiers dying from exposure as they were forced to make camp without putting up their tents. The soldiers had to endure being picked off by snipers, constant ambushes and their officers being tricked and fooled by local tribesmen, who'd not forgotten past battles. Eventually the decimated garrison had no other choice but to make a last stand; this is known as the Battle of Gandamack. They did not stand a chance and were all killed. The Afghans let one man live, Surgeon William Brydon, telling him "go back and tell them this is what happens." The newspaper reported of Brydon's entry into the city of Jalalabad,

He seemed more dead than alive but, when asked 'Where is the Army?', Assistant Surgeon William Brydon managed to reply: 'I am the Army.' [17]

In Jalalabad the past has not gone anywhere. The first time I went to Jalalabad had been by four wheel drive, and we'd driven over the Silk Road – basically a dirt track with a thousand foot drop off to the side –– weaving in and out of Afghans with millennia old eyes staring at us wondering what fresh hell we were bringing. Why was I doing these things? Well I suppose I was the one they asked. I just did what was expected. I went where I needed to go.

When we were doing a major development, expanding the network down in Kandahar, the local village elders wanted to meet a senior executive from the company. Who were the local elders? Well supposedly it was not the Taliban, but it was really. Local representatives representing the Taliban. Around half the villages were back under Taliban control at this stage. I met with the village elders and we negotiated our tower locations. They allowed us to build our towers when we suggested that we would hire our security guards locally. A cell site was a mobile phone tower with two generators, a mast and a BTS[18] on top of it. The site provided mobile phone coverage for the surrounding areas. The management came up with the clever idea, instead of hiring outside security to guard the towers, we'd employ locals. Typically we would employ six or seven guards from that village – generally relatives of the village elders. Everyone was happy. As I was an Irish citizen, it was viewed that I should help with those delicate negotiations rather than the Americans or British. After all, how could they know I once guarded the Queen?

---

17 Kyle, T., 2013. Incredible Story of the British soldier who was the only survivor of a 19th century conquest - and the warnings for today's military missions.. *The Daily Mail,* 25 March.
18 Base transceiver station, a giant dish.

However, in 2007 the Americans took out a Taliban commander with a cruise missile; they tracked him and located him using his satellite phone. The cruise missile landed in his living room, killing him and a few members of his family. As a result of this the Taliban contacted all the operators and told us we had to close down all our towers in the evenings. We couldn't do that as it would have resulted in a massive loss of revenue, evening is the busiest time for phone calls. In that region the other mobile operators employed foreign security firms to guard their towers. Many of their towers were attacked and destroyed, our towers were left alone. The mobile sites were a serious source of revenue for those villages and they protected them as such.

Some villages were Taliban and some were under the protection of a local warlord. The only recourse we had to navigate these relationships was to employ the local guards. The Taliban did try once to attack one of our towers, but the villagers confronted them and told them to leave the tower alone. The Taliban refused so every villager came out, told the Taliban that this was an income for the whole village, warned the Taliban if they did anything the villagers would tell ISAF exactly where their secret crossings into Pakistan were. Our towers carried on functioning, it was a great victory for them and for us as we were able to continue operating. But by me saying *villagers*, don't ever get the impression these people were shrinking violets. This was Afghanistan. Everyone is armed and the whole country was designed by their God as a death trap.

Most Afghans just want to survive their impossibly difficult lives. Unfortunately various and numerous parties, including the Western powers, seem to like "interfering". The Afghans could be forgiven for thinking they have seen it all before. Mainly because they have.

Afghans have been invaded by Alexander the Great; Genghis Khan; the Persians, numerous times; the British Empire a few times over the last couple of hundred years; The Soviet Union; and, of course, now NATO, the Americans and ISAF. So maybe we should cut the Afghans some slack in their distrust of us foreign devils.

Chapter 21

DIALLING IT IN

My driver and friend Rafiola had been with me from the start, I called him the Transporter after the Jason Stratham character from the movie, which he liked. We all had Toyota Prados with government number plates and a siren. The Kabul traffic was mustard, medieval vehicles and modern attitudes. The Transporter would call for me every day, sticking his head over the balcony announcing himself with a "Top of the morning to you Sir, *céad míle fáilte.*" I used to teach him these and other Irish phrases on our long drives up country. I'd laugh, he always wore a Guinness cap and the car would sparkle. I'd already given him a couple of army tips about driving around the city. Rafi would often turn on the siren when we got stuck in traffic As things in Kabul got worse I had to ask him to stop, explaining that drawing attention to ourselves could get us killed. I outlined how important it was to always leave at least a car's length in front to enable evasive manoeuvres to avoid kidnapping and attack. And most importantly not to follow convoys of American military vehicles as they were primary targets, following them could result in being caught in the melee, despite it being an effective way to cut through traffic.

Over the years when we had time and were out in the countryside, I taught Rafiola everything I'd learned in the military. Later on when things got heated in Kabul again, much to his chagrin, I asked him to stop washing the Prado and to remove the siren completely. He protested he'd get in trouble with the transport manager, but I squared that up. A clean vehicle with a white face in it was a lightning rod for trouble. Blending in and being inconspicuous was the name of the game from then on. Rafi was a good friend by the time I left. At least I left him a seriously good driver and with a deadly nickname.

Once the Taliban found out our rural employees worked for an American owned company, some quit, but the majority simply never went home. They didn't get to see their families for years: a serious hardship for an Afghan. The Afghans I worked with or knew did not want the Taliban to come back, but on the other hand they were not keen on what was happening at the time either. The West had come in, corruption was rife, a small coterie of wealthy Afghans were making a fortune but the average Afghan's life hadn't changed. The only thing that had changed was that there was more freedom, especially for women – girls could go to school. Although Afghans were not comfortable with the way things had gone, they certainly did not want to see things go back to the way they were. They also did not hold with foreigners in general being involved in the running of their country.

The man who ran the Herat office near the Iranian border was called Engineer Sali. If you had a degree in Afghanistan your title was "Engineer" plus your name. Engineer Sali worked right through the Taliban reign. When we were travelling around Herat Province, he would regale me with outlandish yet serious stories.

"You know they used to have the check point here."

"What check point?" I replied.

"The beard check point, coming out of town the Taliban would stop you and check your beard length, they would measure it and examine it for signs of trimming. If they suspected anything they would make you get out of your car and a Talib would comb the beard holding a white handkerchief underneath and if any hair fell out that meant you had trimmed your beard. Once you were found guilty they would beat you with sticks, shave your head, throw you in the back of a donkey cart and put you in jail for two weeks."

"Then they had other checkpoints," Engineer Sali continued.

"What were they checking?" I admit I found it morbidly fascinating,

"Well they could stop you and order you to pray, make you get out of the car and recite the Koran. If you failed to do this you would be beaten with sticks, head shaved, thrown into a donkey cart then jailed."

Engineer Sali had lived through those times and he used to laugh about it, despite there being a more deadly side. The reason the checkpoints came up, was we were at Islam Qala on our way from Herat to the Iranian border when we suddenly came across this amazing Mosque in the middle of nowhere. They used to have the checkpoints outside the Mosque. We did a lot of business on the Iranian border; there was only one mobile operator in Iran and calls were very expensive. Iranians would cross over and buy our sim cards. We made good money in the border region.

Satellite phones are vital in a country with a topography and geography such as Afghanistan. Large swathes of Afghanistan are not within distance of a tower and have zero GSM coverage. We had NGOs, American Military, ISAF and embassies as customers who wanted to be able to use the standard Afghan Wireless mobile network and to have their phones automatically switch to a satellite signal if they moved out of GSM coverage. The handset would have duel sims enabling an easy switch. The service provider was a UAE company known as Thuraya, owned by telecommunications giant Etisalat. The now infamous New Ansari was the sole licensed provider for Thuraya phones in Afghanistan at the time.

Telephone Systems International had obtained a satellite licence in the US in its own name before I arrived. TSI was our New Jersey based parent company. Not foreseeing a problem, we shipped about five hundred satellite handsets to Afghanistan, with a value of $1m. But we couldn't get them out of the airport, because Afghan Wireless itself had not acquired the satellite licence for Afghanistan. Despite TSI being our parent, the Afghan authorities insisted we did not have a licence to sell satellite phones in Afghanistan. So the satellite phones were stuck in customs, even baksheesh couldn't get them out, which was a first. This should have been our first warning that more important players than us were lurking in the background.

Why was this such a problem? At the time in question the company that held the Thuraya licence for Afghanistan was called New Ansari Ltd. New Ansari was the sole distributor of

Thuraya satellite phones in Afghanistan. Kirk Meyer, former director of the Afghan Threat Finance Cell, states that New Ansari in its various guises *"was born from the narcotics trade, was heavily involved in the laundering of drug proceeds, had links to the Taliban, and supported numerous corrupt government officials."*[19] These facts had not been established yet, however this was Afghanistan and everybody suspected. In January 2010, US treasury officials raided the offices of New Ansari and in February 2011 they placed it on a blacklist, forbidding any US citizen or company to have any dealings with it. Hence a number of our customers were reluctant to buy satellite phones from New Ansari, as the company's offices had already been raided.

The NGOs, the embassies, the Americans and ISAF all knew what the dogs in the street knew, so they wouldn't buy the Thuraya handsets from New Ansari. The rumours were, and in Afghanistan there is never any reason not to believe rumours, that the satellite phone top up cards were being used to wash drug money out of the country. I never saw any proof of this but it later transpired to be true. Moreover, it was only a minor aspect of the New Ansari operation. Bottom line, Afghan Wireless's customers were not about to buy phones off a drug money laundering operation if they could help it. We needed to find a solution.

Then there was Akram – an Iraqi who'd left Iraq for Canada years previous and now was back cutting deals and doing business in Dubai. He was a real wheeler dealer, who wore a dish dash all the time. He loved the whole Emirati look. We met with him numerous times, expressing our concern that we still didn't have a satellite licence in Afghanistan. He assured us that he could get us a deal. I travelled over to Akram in Dubai to fix the problem.

19 Freeman, M. F. & Kator-Mubarez , A., 2014. *KIRK MEYER, FORMER DIRECTOR OF THE AFGHAN THREAT FINANCE CELL.* [Online] Available at: https://globalecco.org/kirk-meyer-former-director-of-the-afghan-threat-finance-cell [Accessed 29 April 2015].

Akram and I met with the Thuraya management team in Abu Dhabi. We had the meeting, and I was given a verbal agreement from them that they would give us our own licence. I came out of the meeting believing that we had a deal. For Akram this was also good news as we were going to buy all of our top up cards from him.

On our two hour drive back through the desert, as we were basking in the minor glory, Akram told me,

"I have often heard of the white man who could sell sand to the Arabs, now I can say that I have truly met him." We laughed.

He confided in me that he liked a drink and "I also like something else too." My mind boggled with a plethora of sexual scenarios,

"O yeah?

"I like pork." Then we were both laughing.

"Do you?" I said between the tears.

"Very very tasty." He confirmed.

When we arrived back to Akram's office, Thuraya had sent me an email informing me we would not be given the licence after all. I rang, but whatever chance we had was gone. They were in no mood to change their minds.

"Are you mad? You are losing so much business." I tried everything. But they wouldn't budge.

In the end we had to off load the handsets. Thuraya stuck with New Ansari who it seems was keeping everyone very happy.

The deal disappeared like sand through my fingers. The joke on me.

Chapter 22
KABUL BANK AND A BUSTED FLUSH

Among the countless tales of corruption in Afghanistan, Kabul Bank stands out as being a true representation of the extent to which the Afghan people have been robbed by their own leaders.

The first time I encountered the flamboyant banker Sherkhan Farnood was when I bumped into Kamal, our CFO, in Kabul Bank. Afghan Wireless employees, along with most of the country, were paid through Kabul Bank. I was brought upstairs with Kamal and into a room three or four times larger than any office I've ever seen in my life. The walls were lined with chairs according to the Afghan custom. The room was so large that perspective was difficult. In the middle of the room was a desk. Wow, you could have landed a helicopter on it with ease. A beautiful large leather chair, trying to swallow the desk was on the other side. The man sitting somewhere in the chair was Sherkhan Farnood; former professional poker player, winner of the World Series of Poker Europe in 2008 and founder of Kabul Bank and Shaheen Exchange.

Sherkhan had worked for the communists in Afghanistan then fled when they were overthrown. When he was in Moscow in the eighties and nineties he operated Hawalas, the ancient Islamic money transfer system that transfers money without actually moving it. These Hawalas were used to funnel opium and heroin money in and out of Afghanistan and the Soviet Union. Sherkhan Farnood was one of the licensed owners of Shaheen Exchange Hawala, which operated out of Dubai. New Ansari Corporation operated a branch out of Kabul Bank. New Ansari had two branches in Dubai, several others in Asia and Europe and one in California.

The CEO of Kabul Bank was called Khalil Ferozi, a man on paper with no banking experience who'd been involved in playing both sides in the Afghan Civil War, after which he curiously became CEO of the most important bank in

Afghanistan. Khalil Ferozi's past is even murkier than Farnood's. Both Farnood and Ferozi together owned more than half Kabul Bank and were also shareholders in Pamir Airways. A synergy Anglo Irish Bank would have been proud of. According to the Washington Post, "The roots of Kabul Bank stretch back to the Soviet Union. Both Fruzi (sic) and Farnood got their education and their start in business there after Moscow invaded Afghanistan in 1979."[20]

I was introduced to Farnood by Kamal and we chatted amiably. When we left Kamal confided in me that Sherkhan regularly flew to Vegas and blew a million dollars. In retrospect this should have been a red flag, maybe a million red flags.

Sometime later, all Afghan Wireless employees were given the option to use a new airline called Pamir Airways for company flights. It later transpired that the food trays on the airline were filled with hundred dollar bills and the pilots were on a bonus package. Normally on flights out of Afghanistan, I would not partake of the inflight meal, I may have been mistaken when flying Pamir Airways. Another positive was that planes were relatively new and not 30 year old death traps.

In 2010, rumours began to circulate that Kabul Bank was under investigation for corruption and fraud – using bank deposits to purchase property overseas, much of which was in Dubai. Having been recently assured of the banks strength by President Karzai, his brother and many others in the crooked administration Afghans had deposited their life savings in the bank. In August 2010, fearing the bank was going to collapse, thousands of worried Afghans rushed Kabul Bank to try and salvage whatever was left of their savings. $300m was withdrawn, said to be a third of the bank's assets. It was only the Afghan Army and the seizure of the Kabul Bank by Da Afghanistan Bank (DAB) that saved the bank from total collapse.[21] Farnood and Ferozi were also removed from their

20 Masterova, A., Partlow, J. & Higgins, A., 2010. In Afghanistan, signs of crony capitalism. *Washington Post*, 22 February.
21 Ellis, E., 2010. Why Farnood was Flushed Out of Kabul Bank. *Euromoney*, 1 November.

positions. Sherkhan Farnood is quoted in an interview, in response to being asked about the Dubai purchases, "What I'm doing is not proper, not exactly what I should do. But this is Afghanistan."

The Afghan elite had bought property all over the world with loans and dubious transfers from Kabul Bank, probably using New Ansari hawalas. The figure bandied about by the Afghan Threat Finance Cell working out of the US Embassy was nine hundred million dollars in cash missing from the bank since the invasion. Most of it suspected to have left the country in the planes or using the Hawalas. Not to mention being well sprinkled around among politicians, to ensure that nobody noticed and that everybody got paid.[22] The world's biggest bank heist was an inside job.

In March 2013 Farnood and Ferozi were sent to prison after being found guilty of theft. According to the BBC *"In addition to the jail sentence, Farnood has been fined $288m (£190m) and Ferozi $530m (£350m) by the Kabul Bank Special Tribunal – the value of the assets they are deemed to have stolen from the bank."* As of today the money they stole has still not been found. It is suspected that what did not leave the country went to the country's small elite. The real figures are lost in the clouds but sure as shooting they are higher than the mooted one billion. According to US officials, the real figure might be higher than $4bn[23]. The sky is the limit with Afghan corruption.[24]

---

22 Filkins, D., 2011. The Afghan Bank Heist. *The New Yorker*, 14 February.

23 Black, B., 2010. Kabul Bank: Where They Don't Fear The Regulators Enough To Even Hide The Abuses. *Business Insider(US)*, 7 September .

24 Quentin Sommerville, *BBC*, 2013. Kabul Bank fraud: Sherkhan Farnood and Khalilullah Ferozi jailed.

Chapter 23

DEAL OR NO DEAL

Late 2007 while at a conference in Dubai, I was approached by two men representing Vtel Holdings, a Middle Eastern investment company interested in buying Afghan Wireless. They were on the acquisition trail. I picked up the phone to my boss in the States. He confirmed that we were interested. We had an initial meeting with the Jordanian based firm, a multi-million dollar business with varied interests ranging from pharmaceuticals to farms in Saudi. This was not the last time I was to come across this extremely successful business family. Initially they seemed keen on buying AWCC. We proceeded to a period of exclusivity of purchase while they conducted due diligence. We met with them again three months later in New York. They put an offer on the table, but the offer wasn't anywhere near the value we placed on the business.

Nothing more happened with Vtel but AWCC had the taste for it now. We went out to the market to have a look around. I was credited with the idea, thus I was given a contract stating that if the company was sold I was to get 2 million dollars. This 2 million was going to put me back where I needed to be.

Wherever that was.

Vimplecom, a large Russian global telco operator stepped into the fold. They moved very rapidly sending a team to do the due diligence almost immediately. A figure of €500m was being bandied about. This would have made all of us very comfortable.

I had returned to Ireland for a week, dreaming of the big payoff, when I received a call out of nowhere from my mother, telling me my Dad had been in a car accident. I'd hardly seen either of my parents for four years. Something that had not really been on my radar was now front and centre and it left me reeling.

The doctors were not happy and they wanted my Dad to go in for more tests. They were worried that he had a lesion or a tumour of some description on his brain and they needed to operate on him, to have a proper look in order to confirm or allay their suspicions. The tests and procedures were set to take place in July of that year, which was a disaster for me as that was the month the Russians were to perform the due diligence. I was one of five who actually knew the business was up for sale. I was also the commercial head of AWCC so I was expected to be in Kabul with the Russians. I spoke to my Dad offering to come home.

"No it is your job, I have Yvonne and Colin with me. You need to focus on your job son."

The surgeon was going to operate to see what was going on and to decide what could be done. I couldn't leave Kabul as I was orchestrating the deal that was going to put me back on top. I was grief stricken, and I was barely able to deal with it. But I had to focus. Despite speaking to him, the night before the operation I was very upset. Mr Mana saw how upset I was and asked me what was wrong. I explained. As I was watching TV later on, that kind hearted man told me he had organised for the imam to mention my father in the final call to prayer of the day. He promised to give me the heads up in time so I could ring my Dad. Later on,

"He is now praying for your father Mr Alan."

I rang Dad as the prayers were being broadcast from the minaret from the next door mosque,

"What's that?"

"Dad that is a mullah/ imam praying for you here in Kabul."

"Is it?"

"Yeah not many people in Birmingham have had a mullah praying for them in Kabul today have they? And certainly not many Catholics."

"That is true son." I could tell he was upset, I was crying and so was he.

He seemed pleased but like anything else with my Dad he did not actually say so. He was a man of very few words when it came to emotions. I found out afterwards from my sister, that he'd spent the rest of the evening telling anyone in the ward that he thought was a Muslim,

"My son has just called me from Kabul, he has his own bodyguards and he just had a mullah praying for me in Kabul. I bet you never had a mullah praying for you in Kabul." The Muslims he met laughed and agreed that yes that was really good, that he had a good son on the other side of the world pulling Allah onside in his battle.

My sister had mentioned that Dad's driving had become a bit erratic, sure enough it was my old man's driving that had given him away. Through one of life's simple ironies it was a minor car accident that revealed the tumour. They performed the operation and did what they could. Afterwards the doctor told him that they had removed as much of the growth as possible, but the operation was only a partial success. He was given two years to live.

This man who loved swimming and golf and the independence that driving gave him, was suddenly told he would not be able to do any of those things. He was a very fit man and loved activity in any form. Dad had stopped drinking when he turned sixty, he had never been much use at drinking anyway. Unfortunately he was one of those people that changed totally after a couple of drinks, very much in the Jekyll and Hyde mould. He devoted his later years to his grandchildren and golf. Or perhaps it was his golf and grandchildren. He was an amazing grandfather who was affectionately known as Granddad Golf.

When Dad heard what the surgeon had to say, he just gave up. He began waiting to die. He sat in the chair asking,

"What's the point?" It was so sad to see it transpire right in front of our eyes.

I thought at the time he would get through it, that he would fight through it. But he didn't really. I saw him as much as I could, but I didn't see enough of him.

I didn't make enough of an effort as I was focused on one thing: the $2million bonus from the sale of AWCC. At that stage certain other things had started to happen in my life as well. In January 2008 I split up with my wife. We knew the marriage was over in 2007, all we did was row constantly, no more trust between us. The love had dissipated as well. A last holiday with the children in Florida made it apparent the situation was getting worse. Florida was our traditional family holiday, we'd been there six times. But we were barely a functioning couple. I didn't have the courage to separate, even though I knew I needed to leave home, I knew the rows were unhealthy for Violet, for me and especially unhealthy for the children.

We muddled our way through one last Christmas and in January I finally moved out. I rented a beautiful seafront cottage in Dalkey and embraced the life of the bachelor. I tended to travel two weeks a month. I was able to do a lot from home. Much of my work was involved with the due diligence, interspersed with regular trips to the USA, Dubai and the UK. Between January and June, all I did was work on the sale. I had a few girlfriends. Meeting women socially was not difficult. Working in Afghanistan meant I was slightly different to a lot of the men women would meet. It gave me something interesting to talk about. I had a great job, plenty of spare cash and a flash pad.

In the early days of single life I went out on dates. When I told women what I did for a living they would be intrigued. There would be the immediate attraction, but I was very immature. I'd rapidly lose interest and I'd then try and put them off me. A classic male tactic, I've since been told. I couldn't see myself settling down with these women. Unlike a lot of guys, I cannot fake feelings I don't have. I was always at fault, I was in essence a 23 year old in a 44 year old's body. I had met my wife at 21, married her at 23, and spent 22 years in that relationship. I was a fish out of water. I was all over the shop emotionally, already beginning a slow downward spiral. The circles were still too big for me to notice but they were there.

Apart from what was happening with my father, I was still hopeful for the future; I continued working on the due diligence. I look back upon it now and I wonder why I was not more aware of how serious my Dad's condition was. I had no handle on his mortality. I knew about the tumour and I understood it, but I guess I believed he would pull through.

I did not want to accept he was so ill.

Chapter 24

REUNION OF OLD FOES

Late summer, early autumn 2008, I was ready to get my life changing bonus. We had everything ready, the share purchase agreements had been drawn up and the due diligence had taken place. For Vimplecom, Afghan Wireless fitted into their global map. Ehsan Bayat owned 78% of the company and the Afghan government the remaining 22%. The whole thing seemed to be a firm reality. Vimplecom had signed a letter of intent. The due diligence had shown up some theft but nothing particularly unexpected. In an environment such as Afghanistan you always had to manage it. You kind of did your best.

The irony was rife, we were in a post-Taliban Afghanistan. The Russians had invaded in 1980. When they went home they left Naji Buller in charge to run a semi-communist government. A fifteen year civil war followed that even for war hardened Afghans destroyed their souls and their faith in anything other than autocracy, stability and order. The Taliban filled that vacuum. After the Taliban took control they marched into the UN compound where Naji Buller had been given protection and took him. Naji Buller was executed, hung from a police sign post in Kabul. But that was then. The Russians were back and we were selling them Afghan Wireless and nobody batted an eyelid. The Taliban were back as well. It was a reunion of old foes.

This irony was brought into sharper focus one day during the due diligence when I brought Vimplecom's technical team up to the Salang Pass. The Salang Pass is a road with a 14km long tunnel built by the Russians to protect their convoys. Back in the seventies and the eighties when the Russians occupied the country they would send in convoy after convoy along the Salang Pass and they would be picked off by the Mujahidin fighters. There are famous ITN news clips of Russian tanks, trucks and soldiers being blown off the road by the Mujahidin. To prevent such losses, they built the Salang Pass tunnel to go through the mountains rather than over them.

The Russian head of security from Vimplecom was standing on top of the Salang Pass, musing over how he could not believe he was back there after all these years. He'd been down in the Salang Pass as a young soldier and now he had returned. The area around there is a dusty metal graveyard of tanks and aircraft from whichever war you care to mention. Gunships and Hind Ds from Charlie Wilson's war, T72 tanks left by the Russians.

Afghanistan could be forgiven for not believing a word that any invader, pacifier or rescuer tells it. The Afghans had painted over Russian vehicles with Islamic symbols to ensure their message was loud and clear. The painted vehicles were testimony to lots of things. The Afghans had seen and heard it all before. The odd forgotten Hammer and Sickles on otherwise stripped mechanical carcasses, proof that neither communism nor capitalism could really understand or defeat the Afghans. A country designed by their god for guerrilla warfare and a people who are in no rush. The Afghans know, like Ho Chi Minh, that you can't stay forever. Whoever you are.

One of the guys who worked with me, a truly wonderful man, was a Hazara by the name of Engineer Abrar. Hazaris have a very distinct look about them and they are the descendants of the Mongol Genghis Khan. In the Afghan hierarchy, despite their lineage, Hazaris rarely rise to senior positions as they are considered very much a downtrodden people. The Pashtun would always regard themselves as above the Hazaris.

Engineer Abrar had become a great friend of mine and was a lovely man. He had lived through the full gamut of recent Afghan history. When the Russians and Naji Bullah were in power, he'd joined the communist party. When Kabul fell to the Taliban, he had to flee. He went to live in Moscow for a few years as a refugee and spoke fluent Russian.

I thought he was great. When I'd tried to promote him in 2006 I was informed that was not possible as he was Hasari. At the time I'd only been in Kabul a short time and I was not aware of the tribal cultural hierarchies yet. I got around it by giving him extra responsibility. Engineer Abrar started going to the regions and running sales. One day he was involved in a horrific car accident. His driver was killed instantly. Their vehicle overturned and Abrar fractured his right leg. He was taken to a hospital in Kabul. Abrar was a diabetic and the hospital didn't monitor his blood sugar levels properly, which resulted in some kind of blood poisoning setting in. Tragically this meant they had to amputate his good leg, his left leg. He was left with a very badly fractured right leg after his left leg was amputated above the knee.

I felt dreadful, almost responsible, and I knew that in the ultra-violent world of Afghanistan, Engineer Abrar was barely even a number in that hospital. I put a call into my CEO that probably saved his life, otherwise he would have fallen through the cracks of a broken system. Together with the CEO stateside, we were able to get him a lot of support. We had him transferred to a better hospital, this was no small thing in the scheme of things and we also had his salary delivered to his home.

The tragedy was compounded by his wife already being an invalid, paralysed down one side due to a mortar falling on her, close to her family home during the Afghan Civil war. Once Engineer Abrar felt strong enough we sent him to India to get a good prosthetic leg, paid for by AWCC, followed by a desk job. This was not a one way street. In many ways he'd been my right hand man, had always kept an eye on me making sure I never got myself in too much trouble. I did my best for him as he had my back. I relied on him especially in the early days when I was pitted against the Frenchman.

Vimplecom believed that Afghan Wireless fitted into their portfolio and more importantly their global strategic map perfectly. They owned mobile phone operators all over Russia, Georgia, Uzbekistan, and Kazakhstan. Afghanistan was another piece in their regional jigsaw.

I returned to Ireland to finalise my divorce from the woman I had been with half my life, only to discover that Violet had a new man. I was 43 and we'd been together 22 years. We have three beautiful children. This discovery brought me down and despite the naked hypocrisy of the whole situation, I still could not bear to think of someone else being with her. I did not deal with it very well. I understood how ridiculous I was being, but I could not handle thinking about it for months. The main reason, apart from anything else, was my own dysfunctional relationships, which sullied how I saw anyone else's. I got over it eventually. I realised I was still in love with Violet deep down but that was an utterly pointless and self-defeating notion.

I was beginning to disconnect.

My brother Colin, and my sister Yvonne and I should have realised the severity of our Dad's brain tumour, but we were in a form of denial. None of us could reconcile the fit and healthy man our father had been with the idea of him only having two years to live.

My Dad was trying to cope with his illness, he tried his best to fight it. He still couldn't play golf or drive. None of us know what being in that situation feels like, how we would react, what we would do. But he was trying his best and showing some fighting spirit.

Chapter 25

WHAT COULD GO WRONG?

Friday the 5th of September. 2008

I bought myself a top of the range four wheel drive and a new horse on the basis that I was about to get a big bonus. I had two horses in livery, the three children in private schools; I was supporting one home, and living in another. Everything was wonderful. My ex-wife was happy, I was happy. Life was great. I was debt free.

As far as I was concerned, life was trundling along just fine. I am sure there were signs but I cannot for the life of me remember what they were. I woke up on my 44th birthday, September 2008, to a wonderful feeling of excitement, that life was back on track . Everything felt great, what could go wrong? But six months down the line the answer turned out to be: every single thing. I remember that feeling of everything moving in the right direction. Even my Dad's illness, I felt he was dealing with it; although maybe I was in denial.

I wasn't to have those feelings of positivity and progress again until 2011.

In October 2008, I was sitting in the CEO's office in the States. He was discussing what he was going to do with his bonus after the sale went through. How much he was going to donate to his church was uppermost in his mind. Earlier that week, Lehman Brothers had collapsed and suddenly things were looking bleak. I asked the CEO if he was worried about this. He replied,

"Why would I be worried, this will not have any effect on us," he assured me.

"But they are talking about this global recession. Back in Ireland everybody is talking about the economy falling apart." I persisted.

"Yeah OK things are not good, but these guys are Russians. Their economy is booming."

I suppose I was somewhat placated but really deep down I knew. I began to recognise what I could sense, but not yet see: the cold shadows in the distance.

We had been due to seal the deal at the end of October, but there was no word. Early November, Vimplecom pulled out saying they didn't want to borrow the money with the world in so much tumult. At first they didn't pull out entirely, they merely said the deal was on hold and that they were understandably worried. But eventually just before Christmas Vimplecom fully withdrew and made their mergers and acquisitions team redundant. The dream was over. It was on the face of it a reasonable decision. Vimplecom were going to have to borrow a lot of money and were worried that with the global economy collapsing their borrowing capabilities would be restricted. That this would affect the funding of their current business.

For me it felt as if they had taken my future plans and burnt them in front of me.

We got together in the office in New Jersey and everyone was stunned. There was consensus that we had come this far and needed to carry on. I was tasked with finding another buyer, all of us satisfied in the notion we had a very valuable asset and that there was someone out there to buy it. I made several approaches. I was looking for the right prospective buyer. I knew that Zain, a major Middle East operator based in Kuwait, had money to spend and that Afghan Wireless fitted into their footprint.

The weekend I got the phone call from my sister, I had just spent the night at a fancy dress party at Castle Leslie, Glaslough, Co Monaghan. On that truly amazing night I met Sir Jack Leslie and his niece Samantha. Sir Jack Leslie has led a truly remarkable life: captured at Dunkirk, prisoner of war for five years, never married, famous for going to rave parties while he was in his nineties. He is 98!

Castle Leslie itself was a magical place. I went dressed as a Talib. I remember telling Sir Jack Leslie that I had been stationed in the North of Ireland, that I'd protected Lord Caledon. The

Caledon estate is directly next to Castle Leslie. Of course Sir Jack knew Lord Caledon very well and it all added together to one of those wonderful nights, when the past, the present and the future seem one and everything we say seems important. We got a tour of Castle Leslie and Sir Jack himself told us all the ghost stories of the place. The fantastic band only added to what was one of the best Halloweens I've ever had.

I received a phone call from my sister telling me Dad had been admitted into hospital. I flew over. It was around the third or fourth of November. They were still running tests but the surgeon told him that he had six months to live. The surgeon elaborated telling him that when they had a further look the cancer had spread.

My Dad sat there and just said, "Thanks for telling me."

He didn't shed a tear.

Dad only looked at me and said,

"Well that's it isn't it? I'm bollixed", a classic Dublin saying.

"Come on Dad, you can fight this."

"No son, that's it, lights out. I just got to accept it."

We'd always had a strained relationship ever since I was a child. I'd never been that close to him. He was much closer to my sister and very close to my younger brother. I was closer to my mother and my grandmother. Dad was an unusual man, although for his time he was the same as a lot of Irish fathers. He had never been a loving man. No matter what I had done in life, at school, winning gold medals, whatever I had achieved, he'd never once told me he was proud of me. I always kind of resented that. To have heard those words from him would have meant the world to me.

I asked to speak privately with the nurse and we found a quiet corner. I urged him to tell me straight,

"What are we dealing with here? I need to know because I need to tell my brother and sister."

He told me and I'll always remember his vivid description,

"It will be like a computer shutting down. His body will eventually start to shut down piece by piece. He will lose the use of his limbs, and he will end up in a vegetative state and eventually his organs will shut down. He'll live for about six months. He could live a bit longer but not much."

"Thanks for being so honest." I could barely see through the torrid image imprinted on my mind and the tears. I had to compose myself before I went back into Dad.

I told my brother and sister but not my old man. And that was it. They discharged him. All they could offer him was palliative care. They promised to make him as comfortable as possible so that he wouldn't be in any pain. I flew back to Dublin and I felt completely and utterly gutted. I had to carry on. Keep the ship afloat. I was still whistling that same tune, although more and more off key.

In December in Dubai, I met the head of mergers and acquisitions (M&A) for Zain. They were very positive and for them cash was no problem. I introduced the head of M&A to my CEO. We signed an agreement. They received the due diligence pack and came back in January saying they were very interested.

We got to January and my Dad was losing the use of his legs. Things were not good. I didn't want to travel. The Americans said they could not pay me if I was not in Kabul. We compromised and I accepted a reduced salary to spend more time with my father. Financially I was not worried as I knew I had the big payday coming. I'd begun to realise that I'd come to the end of my time in Afghanistan. My personal issues coupled with the increased danger over there, in addition to the relentless near misses in the planes, which had fatigued me and had caught up with me. After five years, I was tired of Kabul and ready to make a break. I had so many other things going on I could not even think about Afghanistan and its spectrum of dangers and mistrusts.

My Dad was in a hospice at this stage. He was so very ill and it was felt the hospice was the best place for him. My mom had started to look after my Dad despite them having separated more than twenty years before. My parents had split up when I was seventeen. When my Dad was in the hospice I'd see them together and it was like they'd never been apart. While they weren't exactly laughing and joking, they were still to my eyes a couple, still Mum and Dad.

One day I was watching my mum mopping his brow.

I said to her, "Mum, you know he never stopped loving you." She started crying.

"Why did he never tell me that?" she replied.

I've always believed Dad had never fully recovered from the break-up of their marriage, that he'd always loved my mother. When she was caring for him towards the end, you could see that there was still a love of sorts between them. It was one of the saddest things I've ever had to witness. But also beautiful at the same time.

Chapter 26

THE END OF ALL ROADS

The Zain deal looked all set to go through by the end of the month. It was the second week of February and I was in the UK visiting my Dad. He was exceptionally ill by this stage. His body was closing down.

I got a phone call from the head of M&A in Zain. He simply said,

"We are pulling out."

"What?"

He confirmed,

"Yes we are pulling out. We have been made aware of a pending legal action and have decided to withdraw from the process."

Boom.

I picked the phone up immediately and in complete shock, phoned my CEO in the States. He said,

"I haven't got a clue what they are talking about."

I replied somewhat taken aback and very miffed.

"Well they've obviously found something."

"Leave it with me." He replied.

That was it. Irrespective of whatever my boss unearthed, Zain had pulled out. While Zain pulling out would have huge repercussions for me, I was completely focused on my Dad. My old man was my only real concern.

Unbeknownst to us, two British men, Stewart Bentham and Lord Michael Cecil, who had been involved with setting up AWCC had heard of the potential sale. Bentham and Cecil had discovered through their contacts that Afghan Wireless was to be sold. They were about to take a case in the English High Court in April 2009, which they would lose in a July 2011 Court of Appeal ruling[25]. The mere insinuation of an ownership issue

---

25 Hastings, P., 2011. Telephone Systems International and Ehsanollah Bayat Defeat US$400 Million Claim Brought by Lord Michael Cecil, Stuart Bentham and Alexander Grinling Bringing 9 Years of Litigation to a Close, *London: PR Newswire.*

raised a lot of red flags for Zain and they decided to pull out. All this came out over that February and March. The details of the case did not matter to me or to Zain, the only thing that mattered was that they were out.

Nonetheless, I could think of nothing else except that my father only had weeks to live. I was full of remorse that I'd seen him so little the last four years. While I had been away in Afghanistan I'd been focused on my job. I was in a constant state of anxiety about the imminent death of my father. Despite the huge impact the acquisition falling through was about to have on my life, I only cared about my old man.

Friday night March 9th 2009, my father passed away peacefully in his sleep. I was home in Dublin with my youngest son when I got the call. My Dad had passed away with my brother, my sister and my mother at his bedside. I'd made a mistake I have been unable to shake to this day. I was supposed to go over that weekend but had changed my mind because my son was playing in the school orchestra on the Saturday. I'd wanted to be a part of that. My sister and I'd both believed he would survive another week or two, which was the advice we had received from the medical team, but he didn't.

I phoned my Violet. I wanted us to get together as a family. But the marriage was over and it was not realistic. I phoned my girlfriend, but she couldn't make it. I felt dreadfully alone. Through timing and life, neither of the women in my life were able to give me much solace. I was at an incredibly low ebb and no one was there for me. There in my house with my ten year old son, I sat there watching TV completely miserable – the most alone I have ever been. Violet picked up Connor the next day and I flew to Birmingham. I dealt with it myself.

That was it. My father William Joseph Barry was dead.

When someone dies in the UK, as opposed to in Ireland, it takes a long time to bury them. And so it proved we had to wait nine days before we were allowed to give him the send-off he deserved.

We buried him on the 18th of March 2009.

I brought Nathan, Catherine and Connor over for the funeral in St Gerard's Church, followed by reception in the Irish Club, or as we knew it, The Paddy's. We celebrated his life with a proper traditional Irish funeral. When my father was young in Dublin, he used to sing professionally in the ballrooms. He sang all the old Frank Ifield and Slim Whitman songs. According to family lore, this was how he'd met my mum. The man who did the Karaoke in the Irish Centre approached me and said he'd always really liked my Dad and would like to look after the music on the day free of charge; we happily accepted this. It was a lovely touch that added something further to the day. My sister, my brother, myself and all his grandchildren, nieces and nephews got up and sang songs to celebrate his life.

Everybody gave him such an incredible send off, very near to where I grew up as a child. I have many happy childhood memories of St Gerard's over the years. I smiled through the tears thinking back to the time I was on leave from the Guards Depot in my Grenadier Guards' uniform and I'd walked into The Paddy's.

Me wearing my peak cap and smart number 2 dress caused a row between my Dad and an armchair Provo. During their row, I'd been drinking at the bar with my friends but I could see Dad involved in a heated altercation with someone he knew. Afterwards I'd asked my old man what was said. Apparently the man had been an acquaintance of my Dad's, he'd told Father ,

"It is disgraceful and inappropriate that your son's walked in here with a British Army uniform on. Disgraceful."

My Dad had turned round and asked him straight out,

"Where are we? Yes that's right we're in Birmingham. Aren't we?" and the guy had said,

"Yeah, so?"

"If my son wants to walk in here in his army uniform let him. You are over here taking your Queen's shilling same as the rest of us. You've made Birmingham your home. If you really feel that way, then move to Belfast and live up there. Don't be bringing that type of shit over to Birmingham."

The argument had ended on that nonviolent impasse.

Dad had looked me up and down, shook his head and asked,
"Did you really have to come in here in your uniform?"
I'd laughed,
"You're an awful little bollix at times." he'd said laughing.
He was right, I was a little bollix.

My Dad's sisters had come over from Ireland for the funeral
and in total over a hundred people attended. I know that he
would have liked it. Surrounded by family, friends and music in
Birmingham, that English city he had carved out a bit of Ireland
in, that had embraced him as one of its own. We all came to say
goodbye to William Joseph Barry.
Goodbye Billy. Goodbye Dad. Goodbye Granddad.

Chapter 27

A NEW REALITY

The emptiness from the loss of my Dad began to envelop me. I headed back to Ireland where I went off to see the *Quiet Man* cottage in the West of Ireland. He'd always loved the movie and I thought it was a fitting tribute. I stayed in Ashford Castle. I thought about my father a lot when I was there. I kept thinking about the pub scene in the film when John Wayne starts singing "The Wild Colonial Boy", my Dad's favourite song. That trip was a tribute of sorts to him. I love my rugby, and that weekend Ireland won the Six Nations Grand Slam, March 2009. That amazing Irish performance would have made my old man's day. The culmination of many things made it an emotional weekend. But the culminating was not finished yet.

I came back to Dublin, back to a new reality. My old man was gone and there was no way of getting around that.

My mind was in no place to make any types of decisions. This heralded the real beginning of my problems although I was still relatively oblivious to them. My body and my mind, through the catalyst of events, had begun its own shutdown. All of me needed a break. The sale of the company had fallen through. Violet had filed for divorce proceedings. Financially, I was beginning to find myself under pressure, due to the reduced salary and the amount of time I had taken off work.

Afghan Wireless got in touch and said they needed me back in Kabul immediately. "We are going to see if we can find another suitor, but you need to get back to your day job."

I agreed and I packed my bags. I was to fly back to Afghanistan, despite the deal having been called off and everything being in turmoil. I was flying out on the Sunday and I was shopping on the Saturday with my two sons. On my way home I got a text from Violet.

"I'm away this weekend. You need to be here to look after Conor."

Conor was ten.

I replied, "Well I have to fly out tomorrow."

"Well it's not my problem." She was away for the weekend in Rome.

Reality was I could have done something about it, I had two older children more than responsible enough to look after my son. I sent an email to the company telling them I could not fly Sunday. Told them what had happened, I was in no mood for Afghanistan.

Afghan Wireless were not happy but they said, "OK, fly next week". The Thursday of the flight came round. I could not face it. I said to myself, I am not going. I was beginning to realise the truth, I was never going back Afghanistan. How the hell could I?

I sent an email and resigned from my job. It had started with an excuse, which eventually turned into my resignation. I was divorced, fatherless and unemployed. I am not sure what I was thinking. I did not have much money in the bank. I had massive commitments from all elements of my life, family finances and personal finances; I had debts, financial and emotional, that were all coming due. I had no way of paying any of them.

What followed was a year of my life when I went completely and utterly off the rails. I did nothing but drink, party and play sport; I paid barely any bills. I lived on my wits despite the fact that I was completely witless. Every now and again, Afghan Wireless gave me some consultancy but I was nowhere near paying my way.

So everything that happened was my fault and I take full responsibility.

Chapter 28

SPORTS THERAPY

I first started show jumping with Violet in the local riding club after we moved to Ireland. I'd never been on a horse in my life prior to that. Both of us immersed ourselves in equestrian sport for the next ten years. Over time instead of it bringing us together it drove us further apart. My desire and need to keep proving myself annoyed my wife more and more. Instead of it becoming an enjoyable couple's pastime, a sanctuary from the outside world, it became the manifestation of my unremitting desire to win. And of course in the long term I only really lost.

If I could relive the past I would stop myself from ever getting on a horse. I know it's a folly to ever regret the past and I don't, except for my equestrian hobby stroke obsession. I can think of very few people I met during those ten years from the so called horsey set that I would keep in my life, besides our four horses that is. In my experience, the show-jumping set are the greatest bunch of back-stabbing poisonous oddities one could ever meet. The animals tend to be lovely and the humans the complete opposite. They are truly a bizarre bunch of closed minded, weird and curious individuals best left to themselves.

From the outset the show-jumping set loathed me. They regarded me as new money. – as someone who had no talent. But what really infuriated them was that I actually won rosettes. In the beginning I hadn't a clue what I was doing and I was very fortunate to have found a horse as good as the King. He was a fabulous horse. The King was my school master, he taught me and enabled me to compete way above my level. This infuriated them because they wanted to keep me beneath them. That was where they believed my level was.

When I was not winning, they said it was because I was a useless rider. When I eventually started winning, they said it was because I had a great horse. When I kept winning, they said I was destroying the horse. I couldn't win with them really. I am not sure now why I ever tried or cared. My competitive nature never sat very well with any of them. Every time I jumped everyone wanted me to fall off and fail. After I fractured my femur in 2002, I was back on a horse within 6 months. It was complete madness, absolutely crazy to get back on a horse so quickly, my leg was so weak I couldn't even grip properly. If I had fallen off the horse again I could have ended up in a wheel chair. What was I trying to prove and to whom?

This is my favourite joke, and one that goes a long way towards explaining the Irish culture of begrudgery that I encountered in the Irish horse riding set:

An American comes to Dublin and arrives to stay in Dalkey. He strolls contentedly down to Bullock Harbour. The fishing boats are coming in and they are pulling all these very large lobsters out of the boat. There are big crates full of these lobsters lined up all along the harbour. The American eyes them and says

"Wow they sure are fabulous lobsters." In his long American drawl.

The fisherman replies, "Thanks aye, they are the finest Irish lobsters, fresh from the Irish sea, the best lobsters in the world."

The American noticeably enthralled says, "Wow they really are amazing. You have a full crate of them there, watch, that one on top is about to crawl out."

The fisherman looks at him confused with his eyebrows raised and tells him seriously, "Didn't I just tell you they were Irish lobsters."

"Well what difference does that make?" the American asks slightly bewildered,

"Well, when one gets on top the rest drag him back down."

This is so true of the Irish and of everyone in the show-jumping world here or abroad. They are all Irish lobsters.

Late 2008, a few months before my Dad died, King was around fourteen and he couldn't jump anymore. Another horse came on the market called Fred and I bought him . By this stage my leg had completely healed. After many lessons and thousands of Euro invested, my riding had come on. I took it seriously and I knew what I was doing.

A few months after my old man had passed away I was competing in a show jumping event. I could see a small group of the riding clique watching and willing me to come off. Was this all in my mind? Sadly not. I wondered to myself, why am I doing this? Why am I spending all this money on a sport with people that I don't even like or want to be around? Fred refused the fence twice, then ploughed through it on the third attempt and off I came, first time since 2002. The poor horse had picked up the negative vibes from me, the way I was and the way my head was, nature mirroring the misfortune of man. I went back, put Fred in the horse box, drove him back to the yard, put him in the field and have never ridden since. The livery contacted me and told me I owed them three months fees.

"Sell the horse, sell the tack, and let me know what's left."

That was it, just like that I was finished with a ten year passion. I haven't been horse riding since and don't have any desire to ride ever again.

I was never suited to the sport. I hadn't been involved in it for long enough before I started competing and I didn't respect it enough. I took it for granted that I would be good at it, when in actual fact I was competing against people who'd been riding since they were children. They used to take one look at me and think,

"Look at that fucking idiot. That English man with all that money. He's a gobshite."

In that miserable year I had after leaving Afghan Wireless and losing my Dad I couldn't face any responsibility. I couldn't deal with anything that involved concentrating. All I wanted to do was feel sorry for myself and drink, I never became an alcoholic thankfully there was still something in me that prevented me from that fresh hell. Instead I threw myself into sport, cycling at first, cycling all day from Dublin to Wexford or Carlow, whichever I reckoned would keep me moving and away from my life the longest. But the cycling was not enough, it was too solitary. It gave me opportunity for reflection, which was an anathema to me then.

I was watching the Dubai Sevens on TV when I decided that I wanted to start playing rugby. I had never played rugby in my life, but I couldn't shake the idea. My local club in Kilternan was called De La Salle Palmerstown. It is known as DLSP. I phoned up the rugby club and simply asked them,

"I'd love to start playing rugby, but I have never played the game before in my life, in school I was more into football. What can I do?"

Gerry, who runs the clubhouse said, "The J4s train on a Tuesday night. If you come down I will introduce you."

I was in a very dark place emotionally, and things were falling apart. But I went up anyway. I dropped the ball more than I caught it, but nonetheless I was welcomed in with open arms: especially in the crunching tackles. I was on the fringe of the subs' bench and that was OK. The players were a mish mash of electricians, guards, lawyers – people from every walk of life. In many ways the club saved me, I found the lads just when I needed them. For the whole of 2009 the club was my life, it was my only real social outlet. Mentally I was numb at best, but the group of guys in the club helped me, mainly by treating me as they would anyone else. They knew nothing about me. They didn't care, which was refreshing and a sanctuary away from the Greek chorus of hate I had begun to hear from other quarters.

Initially, after hearing I had worked in Afghanistan, the rugby team started calling me McNab. That soon changed to The Tan after the Black and Tans. The club has remained an integral part of my life. It has served to be a useful way to spend quality time with my youngest son who also plays for the club. But unlike his father he has talent and good hands. I am very grateful to the club and the friends I have made there.

Next up was boxing, as I continued my bid to exercise away my demons, literally and figuratively. The boxing was great for getting rid of anger and frustration and of course a fantastic way to keep fit. All I wanted to do was keep my mind distracted, and the only way for me to keep it distracted was with sport. I couldn't work, my brain couldn't focus on anything important.

When the rugby season finished, I was invited up to the local boxing club to train and somehow allowed myself to be talked into competing in a white collar tournament. Even more extraordinarily, my planned opponent, a man roughly my own age and ability, pulled out late on and was replaced by a 25 year old lad with a bit about him. I was 45, hanging on by a thread with nothing much about me.

The match was supposed to be an exhibition bout, one of twelve on the night, but I was not in that type of humour. I hadn't been for quite some time. I decided, despite the age and ability gap, to give it every single thing I had. I vowed I would leave it all out there. The first round I charged in like a wild bull, the second round I was somewhat more circumspect, and the third I was punch drunk, I could hardly catch my breath. When the bell rang my opponent came over and congratulated me on a great fight. I have to admit I felt at once like I had been hit by a truck and, despite having lost, that I had won the world championship belt. The following day was a slightly different story as my body screamed at me that perhaps my days of fighting young lads were over.

Sport was all that I could manage and it masked my deteriorating health.

Chapter 29

THE DESCENT

I would like to be able to tell you that I got my act together not long after that, but I didn't, I remained a wreck. I found it very difficult to care about anything and I found little solace except in physically pushing myself. Sports were simply distractions, as more and more little pieces fell off inside and I could not put them back. I came to the realisation after a while, even through the worsening fog, that there was something wrong with me. I went to see my family doctor first who told me he thought I'd had a breakdown.

I was not ready to hear that so on I went.

I was up to my eyeballs in debt, although not as bad as some. From April onwards, I just coasted through life in this dream world I inhabited. I was a completely different person, pretty much the opposite of the person I had been. For want of a better word, I became a real asshole. I didn't take responsibility for anything. I felt detached from everything. I couldn't even read a newspaper. My mind was a blur, it would not let me focus on the print. I knew something was wrong and so did those close to me.

Finally I plucked up the courage and I sat down with a psychiatrist; I had a number of different sessions and for the first time in my life I told someone my life story. Start to finish. She focussed in on the two shooting incidents. This was like opening up Pandora's Box. I broke down. I was at the end of my tether, I simply couldn't control my emotions. I cried uncontrollably. I had been pushing and twisting the memories down into myself for the last twenty three years and never dealing with them. She said to me "Alan you've been suffering from post-traumatic stress disorder, PTSD since the age of 24."

I was not quite sure what she was talking about. "What?"

"Alan you have been dealing with this issue, since you were 24 years of age. And you have lived with it. If we go back over your life and look at your behaviour, we see that you exhibited an unusual lack of fear, a lack of fear that has allowed you to do the work you have done. Particularly in Afghanistan, visiting places like Kandahar, Jalalabad, contemplating killing others to save yourself. Not normal, not how normal people live. You have dealt with it like it was a normal way of life. You have seen things in your military service which people will never see."

"So I was not me, I have just been acting as me?" I only saw negativity.

"I am telling you now from 24 years of age you have had PTSD. This has manifested itself throughout your life in you being a risk taker. Why? Because your body and your mind have never dealt with what happened back then. Since those incidents you have lived on the edge. You have been successful in business, successful in sales. But you have done it because of your tenaciousness. What has come to pass is because of all these things: the death of your father, the loss of your home, the break-up of your marriage after 22 years, the break-up of your relationship, the failure of the sale of the company, the loss of your job. Your body and mind has told you it can't cope with it anymore. In essence you have had a complete and utter breakdown"

The counsellor explained and reiterated that I had been suffering from PTSD and that my life up until then had been overtly affected by it. Now my body and mind were telling me no, no more, they could no longer handle it. As I reflected on this I came to the conclusion that my life had been a lie. Everything I had achieved through me being me, had really not been me. It was all someone else and maybe this fucked up failure is who I really was.

November of 2009. I was:

Emotionally wrecked;

Financially broke;

Psychologically unwell;

Smack bang in the middle of a catastrophic breakdown. I could no more pay a bill than I could go back to work. I was fucked. I was in the wrong place again.

Chapter 30
CRASH LANDING

I opened my eyes and I found myself on top of Killiney Hill in Dublin, an idyllic place that previously had been the scene of some of my happiest moments. I sat slumped on a bench listening to the water and my life stream slowly into the sea. I wanted to dissolve. I tried to find meaning in the stunning view. It was 6am and I was wearing my pyjama bottoms, a t-shirt and trainers. I couldn't sleep and was trying to find peace and tranquillity. I am not sure what drew me to this location. The moon was still out even though it was the break of dawn. I thought to myself, my life is over, this is it. A car would wander past behind me on the Vico Road, the tyres on the fresh morning road giving me something to attach my disintegrating thoughts to. I couldn't imagine how I was going to dig myself out of the unholy mess I had gotten into. My focus was shot to shit. I couldn't face dealing with my problems. I had no fight left inside. I was empty.

If I didn't have children, I think if someone had given me a Glock I would have blown my brains out. In fact I can think of one or two people who would have bought tickets to watch. But the love I have for my children saved me. I couldn't do it to them. The only thing I had remained through my hell was a fully committed and loving father. I knew if I'd done it, I would be at peace, I would be away from all these problems I'd created for myself through my bad judgement, especially that I would be free of the mental torture I was going through at the time. The allure of the peace was strong; how relaxing it would be.

I rang my poor mum. She could hear I was at my wits' end. I broke down and she broke down. She is an old lady and I shouldn't have laid it on her but I was alone. I am not the last man to turn to his mother at his darkest hour. She couldn't handle it either. The transformation from what I had been professionally and personally was a terrible thing for her to witness. The shining light had changed into this blubbering wreck. She was in England and there was nothing she could do for me, but hearing her voice did help. My mother has never judged me and has always been there for me 100%. I got back in the car.

A few hours later, I rang my best friend Mark. He could hear the pain in my voice.

"Where are you buddy?" he asked.

"I'm in Dublin."

"Stay there I am coming over."

That afternoon he phoned me, he was in Dublin. He'd come to find me and, I suppose, to save me.

"Alan you're coming back to the UK with me."

"No I'm not. I have to stay here," For what I had no idea, to watch myself swirl down the drain?

"You are, you're coming back with me. You can't stay here. Come with me, we have to get you right again."

That was it, I went with Mark to England for six to seven months working in his business, putting my life back together piece by poxy piece. Each month I improved. I started flying back to Dublin at weekends to see my children, while getting myself back to normal.

Debt, illness and grief had brought me to Killiney Hill that December morning, unable to face going forward. The culmination of all three had done what the IRA or the Taliban had failed to do, they had taken me down.

Although I was abroad, I could still hear the negative vibes from the mess I had left behind me, I was clearly not far enough away. Stories would work their way back, how my friends had been confronted at parties about their friend Alan, who owed millions. These ridiculous rumours about me were now being spread by people I'd never even met. Classic Irish tales of €10,000 debt growing to €100,000 every time it was told.

Ok, I had spent my days drinking in Bono's local bar until closing, going to house parties, drinking 'til early morning, wiling away the afternoon drinking coffee in cafes; never doing any real work, feeling sorry for myself – yeah I had become that guy. In fact, I was worse, because I was that guy and I was not paying my bills. I'd not been faking it though, I'd been lost. For eighteen months I'd been a broken and very unwell person.

I went to see the local priest. I will never forget the words he told me:

"Life is like a long river, smooth currents and calm waters followed by rough currents and then rapids. You, my son, are in the rapids. Believe me calm waters will come again."

I just had to ride it out.

During my eighteen months of madness, I was determined to shield my children from the issues I was facing. It was my responsibility to tackle my demons alone.

I am still coping with the financial and emotional fallout of that 18 months of madness, of my 50 years on this planet. But now I am dealing with it.

Thankfully the very bottom waned further and further away. Like most fortunate people who survive after hitting rock bottom, I worked my way out of it through the love and support of my family and through working with an old friend. Working with Mark helped me begin to regain my self-esteem and self-worth. The counselling for PTSD also helped immensely. No one can do it on their own.

Let him who is without sin cast the first stone.

Judge ye not lest ye be judged would be my advice to the ghouls out there who tried to have me exiled from my own country and my own life.

My old regimental motto is *Honi Soit qui May y Pense*.

It is Latin for *shame be to he who thinks evil*.

I leave that verse to those who hear it.

Chapter 31

FROM HELL TO PARADISE

I had begun to see light at the end of the tunnel, to use that tired old adage. Tired and true. Through the work and getting paid, I was regaining some element of my self-esteem. I had dealt with all the hell but I was still emotionally scarred.

Back up on LinkedIn, I was approached by a head-hunter called Duncan from RP International, Singapore. He was looking for someone with my background to go to Papua New Guinea and sort out some problems for his client. He wanted a strong marketer to manage a mobile operator that was in a bit of a mess. My remit was also to include a week per month building their sister business in the Solomon Islands.

It was a very well-paid job and gave me my own opportunity to continue rebuilding my life after the kick-start I had from Mark. I completed three successful interviews and was offered the role of Chief Commercial Officer for Bemobile in Papua New Guinea. I would need to move to the other side of the world. Just where I needed to be. There was only one drawback; I would be 24 hours away from my children. But I had no choice. I owed it to them and myself to seize the opportunity and rebuild my life, as they relied on me and I had responsibilities.

I left Dublin in July 2011 and travelled to Port Moresby, the capital of PNG. The first thing I'd been told was the country was rife with random violence, military coups, cannibalism, and car-jackings. But I liked it. After the previous 18 months I was ready for anything. Sure you had to keep your wits about you, but that was always something I had trained into me. OK there were certain parts of PNG that you wouldn't go near, you would probably be shot in the street. Yeah we all lived in a secure compound. White women could not go round on their own. Theft was rife. There was still something about the place that sat well with me. And obviously compared with Afghanistan it was a walk in the park – Afghanistan was back being the most dangerous place on earth after a brief respite. I was glad to have survived my time there. More than anything I could no longer sense the negative vibes from the ghouls that I had brought into my life in Dublin. A negative frame of mind can attract negative people and sadly I was no different to anyone else. It was time to put distance between the ghouls and myself. Even they could not be felt in PNG. My head was thawing out. A new clarity had replaced how I used to feel before I had my breakdown.

I like to think I'd become a better person by then, gone the brashness and a lot of the arrogance of someone who'd always expected everyone else to succeed like they had. My first real experience of having no money had also been a very humbling one. I hope that since my illness I have shown compassion to those who have suffered similar fates. I'd lost respect for myself and I'd lost respect for everything in my life. I realised in PNG that I had self-worth. PNG allowed me to understand and believe I was not a complete failure.

I had always tried my best with my staff and with locals in general. But the breakdown had made me humble; something nobody had ever accused me of before. I was now walking away from those things into a better future. I hoped as the wounds healed that I'd be left with scars to serve as reminders of the virtue of kindness and understanding.

It's true that although it nearly killed me, in the end it made me stronger. Each one of the things I'd had to deal with would have brought a person down, brought them to a breakdown. Never mind all of them at the same time, all at once they were almost cataclysmic.

Time, distance and healing was PNG's first attraction.

To get to PNG, you travel for a full day. Dublin to Singapore takes in total around sixteen hours – then another flight for eight hours.

The capital Port Moresby was not that heavily populated, but it was a very interesting place: a South Pacific island and a serious culture shock. If you are going anywhere serious in PNG, you fly. The islands are full of history and very different tribes. I learnt that people from the Highlands were incredibly aggressive and that was something I'd just have to get used to. There were two main islands

– New Britain and New Ireland. The Sepik people who lived mostly along the coast were different to the Highlanders, much easier to get along with. I took to the place quickly.

We used to fly into the Volcano city Rabaul, the capital of New Britain, in over the Bismarck Sea, so called because PNG had been colonised by the Germans up until the First World War. Rabaul had been destroyed by a volcano in the 1970s and the city moved further along the coast. We flew in through the smoke wafting out of the volcano, which, along with the acrid smell of sulphur, was overpowering. They served to remind me that I was a long way from home, and I was into it.

The Northern Islands were still mostly Lutheran and home to many German graveyards from when they colonised the islands. In 1919 at the Treaty of Versailles, Germany lost all its colonial possessions. After the First World War PNG become an Australian protectorate. During the Second World War, in January 1942, while the bulk of the Australian Army was fighting in North Africa, four thousand Australian reservists and the Papuan Infantry Brigade (PIB) found themselves in a two year siege with the Japanese. The Bomana cemetery outside Port Moresby is full of too old or too young Australian soldiers who'd stood firm against the Japanese attacks, despite taking huge casualties.

The Japanese had invaded the city of Rabaul and New Ireland. The only soldiers the Aussies had left were territorials, mostly reservists, the wrong ages to fight apparently. Along the famous Kokoda trail the Japanese came within sight of Port Moresby, but were beaten back by the supposedly inferior Australian troops and the PIB. The eclectic group of part time and professional soldiers refused to give in and fought to their death. Eventually Australia was able to get regular soldiers there to relieve the worn out depleted force and the Japanese never took Port Moresby.

Independence for PNG came in 1974, and like most new countries it's had its problems. When I arrived the long-time ruler, Sir Michael Sumare, had just been ousted while on medical hiatus in Singapore. He was ousted by a government led by Peter O'Neill. Samare came back putting PNG in the unusual and awkward position of having two governments, two foreign ministers, two everything. Despite some calls for delaying the scheduled election it went ahead and Peter O'Neill is the current prime minister of Papua New Guinea after a failed military coup.

None of these things perturbed me too much, I fell back on the old soldier's adage of being there to do a job. I was up against an Irish owned firm called Digicel , who were and are the market leader and definitely the top dogs. Everybody was in awe of them. Well not everyone, I was happy to have my shot at their title.

Bougainville is the largest Island in the Solomon archipelago and became part of an independent Papua New Guinea in 1975. Bougainville is home to the world famous Panguna Mine. Right from the opening of the Panguna Mine in the sixties there were tensions, violence and conflicts of interest. The mining company Bougainville Copper Limited (BCL); the PNG Government, the landowners on the islands, both in favour and against the mine; the Australian and New Zealand Governments were all involved. The civil war took place from 1988 to 1998 and involved the PNG Army and the Bougainville Revolutionary Army; it is considered the largest conflict in the South Seas since the Second World War, with between 15,000 and 20,000 dead. The dispute over pollution, land ownership and independence all centred around the Panguna mine, which at one stage accounted for 45% of PNGs exports.

A peace deal was signed in 1998 and the ceasefire has largely held. As of the April 2015 the mine has not reopened yet. However, some on the island are calling for the reopening of the mine to help fuel the Bougainville economy. Elections are due to be held later in 2015. There remains some dispute as to whom owns the geological rights on Bougainville. The regional government of the autonomous region Bougainville, and the PNG Government of Peter O'Neill in Port Moresby both claim the rights as their own. [26]

26 Carl, A. & Garasu, L., 2002. Weaving consensus: The Papua New Guinea - Bougainville peace process. *Accord,* Issue 12.

My own business, Bemobile, was in worse shape than the government. It was an expat feeding trough, with inflated bonus structures leading to falsified numbers, up and down the profit and loss account. They had many over paid consultants as well as a convoluted, murky shareholding.

I also had responsibility for the Solomon Islands, a group of Islands that have very little to do with PNG other than Port Moresby being 874 miles away from Honiara, the capital. The Solomon Islands lie to the south east of PNG.

The Solomons have had their own problems, but to look at them, they were a paradise on earth. I was based in Honiara a city on Guadalcanal, the main island. Not so long previously it was the scene of ethnic unrest that ended up with the Solomon government requesting foreign help to resolve the issue. Guadalcanal is an island known for a very famous battle in the Second World War. Following Pearl Harbour, the first battle of the South Pacific between the Americans and the Japanese was fought on the Solomon Islands. The main bay outside of Honiara is called Iron Bottom Sound, because so many ships sank there, and remain there. When we were building our telecoms network across the Solomon Islands, we would come across live ordinance from the Second World War that would have to be dealt with by local specialists.

As well being a historical gem, the Solomon Islands are also a tropical paradise. The water is crystal clear, the tropical fish swim around you. It is a vivid, colourful reminder of the earth's splendour. On the darker side the island is poverty stricken as there are no natural resources there, or more accurately they have not accessed their natural resources. The Solomon Islands are said to have a lot of mineral wealth, oil, gold, gas, but they are all untapped. It has no real economy of its own besides tourism.

When I arrived in PNG, the company was in complete disarray. Bemobile had been the original national telecoms provider before it was privatised.

The primary issue we had in Bemobile, was that three years previously, after privatisation, they'd brought in grossly overpaid expat consultants to set up and run the new firm. These consultants had made a complete dog's dinner of the company. In my professional career I have never come across a mess of such magnitude as I encountered there. I had been recommended to the job by the CFO Andy, an ex-colleague from Afghanistan. Presumably he thought I would be up for the challenge.

I encountered a major contradiction in numbers, which was almost impossible to get my head around at first. However, time would soon give me a clear understanding of exactly what was going. The bonus structure was based on the growth of the company from a subscriber, or an active customer point of view, this is not a good idea any day of the week. All bonuses should be based on revenue and profit. The previous management had indulged themselves in all sorts of shenanigans to achieve perpetual growth in the reported numbers of new users. The real revenue figures and the reported revenue figures were two vastly different numbers; they were strangers that had never met.

The company was owned by the PNG government through a company called the Independent Public Business Corporation (IPBC); the investment arm of the government. IPBC had a representative on the board and a share of the business. The second shareholder was a company called Steamships; a very profitable PNG based property business. The remaining shareholder was Hong Kong Investment Company. A number of people were robbing the business on a monthly, weekly and daily basis. The PNG government via IPBC were becoming more and more disenchanted with what was going on. They had absolutely zero faith in the expat employees or in the management, but they were somewhat hamstrung as the government did not want to give the impression of meddling in private enterprise.[27] (Morauta, 2011)

---

27 Morauta, T. R. H. M., 2011. The theft and waste of public money in Papua New Guinea's Public Enterprises, Port Moresby: *The Ministry for Public Enterprises*.

Chapter 32

WALKING DISASTERS

The first Bemobile CEO I worked with was a man called Patrick, an Irish guy earning $35k a month, spending approximately three days a week in PNG. The rest of the time he would laze around his palatial pad in Cairns Australia. Tuesday morning to Thursday night was his typical working week, doing as little as possible besides informing people how he was only waiting for his bonus. He didn't engage with the staff. I worked with him for approximately four months. In that period of time I had very little interaction with the man, other than listening to him tell me he was only waiting for his bonus and that he was going to leave as soon as he got it.

Any time I went to him with any issues he didn't want to know. The problems would have affected his bonus so he had no interest in addressing them. Whatever about him, he only stayed four more months (he didn't get his bonus but he did get the boot), there was another Irish guy, Brian the COO, doing exactly the same thing; they were a double act. The other fella lived in Brisbane and he was on about $30k a month, so he only did two days a week, flying in Tuesday night and leaving Thursday night.

In the middle of this I was trying to do my job, dealing with massive churn. Why? For nearly a year Bemobile had been falsifying subscriber numbers. What we were reporting as our active customer base, and our actual active customer base were two altogether different figures. We had a really big churn issue, whereby we were losing hundreds and hundreds of customers every month. But we actually weren't; they had never been customers or even people in the first place. Under instruction from the CEO Patrick, the sales department had been sending phones out to retail outlets with the sim cards already connected as if they had been sold to someone already. To add to this, top up cards were not configured properly on the Online Charging System (OCS), the billing platform. Essentially, customers' phone credit sometimes never expired. Finally the OCS billing system was not fully integrated, which resulted in our not being able to bill our customers correctly.

Another problem we had was that in order to show these Monopoly figures the Irish duo had been doing three for one promotions every week for the guts of a year. If you bought ten units you got thirty. This was across the board, one hundred bought you three hundred. So we had a revenue of 3 million Kina[28] a month sitting on our billing platform, which was not real revenue. This revenue did not represent real money, nobody had actually ever spent it, it was no better than Monopoly money.

I uncovered all of the figures. Actually all I did was choose to notice them, everyone else had chosen to ignore them. They were right in front of everyone. I was paralysed with shock and I didn't really know what to do with the problems they were so vast, far reaching and entrenched. After the CEO had told me to mind my own business, I went to see Andy the CFO about this. Luckily at the time the Andy had the ear of the board. The board and the Irish CEO agreed to part company as a result of this.

The Irish CEO and his side kick were removed and Andy was given the CEO job on an interim basis. Andy had a great approach to business and we set about correcting the balance sheet. Despite everything I have said, I wouldn't like to give you the impression that I didn't enjoy my job in PNG. Job satisfaction wise, on a scale of one to ten, it was ten. It was simply brilliant fun and exactly what I needed. We spent our days firefighting and they flew by. Every time we looked at some issue or another it would reveal another mess. I'd never experienced anything like it. Afghan Wireless was an extremely well-run company and had been nothing like Bemobile.

I got a lot of experience going forward. I was suddenly involved in operational issues. Previously I had only been involved in the commercial side: developing customer bases.

---

28 Currency of PNG.

PNG continued to enchant me. Never mind what you hear on the news, it is a wonderful place with beautiful people. I worked a Monday to Friday standard working week. I lived in Port Moresby. We were twelve hours ahead of Europe. When I was getting up my children were going to bed, and when I was going to sleep they were getting up. This oddly was quite conducive to good communication. I spoke to my children five times a week.

In the evenings I lived in a very pleasant gated community. I had a small apartment; access to a gym, a pool, and a bar; and I had my own vehicle. Nobody had a driver and to me some guy waving a knife at me, or threatening to blow my head off for my wallet was no different to being in New York. I wasn't worried. Social life was good. In Port Moresby the local yacht club was the big scene and I joined that. Most of the expats you'd come across were Australian, a lot of them colonial relics, who had lived there their whole lives. A lot of elderly Australian men married to women thirty or forty years younger than them with three or four children. The PNG women obviously looked on the older guy as a safer bet. When an expat married a Papuan woman, they were expected to support the whole extended family.

Many people in PNG drink and drive, or they did then anyway. There was no legislation prohibiting. Expats tended to socialise in the yacht club. It was there that I met Michael, a young Irish man who like me also worked for a multinational. He was a touch the worse for wear leaving the club one particular evening, although none of us really remember him going. Judging from what happened Michael was driving recklessly and probably too fast when he his car overturned at a roundabout. The car finished upside down but he had been wearing his seat belt and thankfully he wasn't really hurt. When he came around the car was surrounded by a group of people. He started to thank them profusely believing them to be coming to his aid.

"Thanks for helping me, you're lifesavers."

Unfortunately for Michael, instead of helping him out of his seatbelt they took his mobile phone, his watch, his valuables, his briefcase, his laptop. They didn't help him out of his seat belt, leaving him exactly where they found him. Weirdly he was still lucky. Lucky to be alive.

Lesson: don't drink and drive.

One of my colleagues in Bemobile at the time was another young man from Ireland. Like most young people he knew absolutely everything and could not be told anything, by anybody. He thought he was a world expert and authority on every subject. From the start we liked to call him the Walking Disaster. He had a South American girlfriend. From the beginning he began to earn his nickname.

On his second day in Port Moresby he left his laptop in the back of his car, something you would not do anywhere on earth. The laptop was stolen, oh yeah, along with his passport, which of course was in the same bag.

Next up for our hero, despite our repeated warnings that certain areas of the city were absolute no go areas, he still always knew better, he still was always right: One evening after football he went to pick up his girlfriend who'd been giving a Spanish lesson in one of the dodgiest parts of town. When he got out of the car to get her, he was approached by three men, one armed with a shot gun. They ordered him to lie on the ground while they car jacked him with a shotgun to his head, warning if he moved he was going to die. His car was used the following day in an armed robbery. They took his wallet and his phone. Then they took his vehicle, his trainers, his clothes; all they left him was his underwear. He was in a place called Six Mile in Port Moresby. We couldn't believe it. We decided it was probably better for all concerned if he left. He agreed for once.

His coup de grace, he booked his tickets to go home via Australia despite us telling him repeatedly that his girlfriend would have visa issues. Luckily for him, he was an expert on international aviation transit law and he ignored us.

He came to the office on his last day and we all wished him the best. He shook all our hands and said his final goodbyes.

Of course he was back two hours later, as he had been refused entry to the flight with his girlfriend due to visa restrictions and had lost his tickets.

We eventually managed to get them both out of the country safely and thankfully they were no longer our issue.

The road to Jalalabad 2007

With guards and Farid the day he drove the French man to the airport

Herat 2008. With two locals and a trophy from the soviet invasion

A deserted Russian airbase, this truly was a ghostly place

Iraq 2012

The Silk road between Kabul and Jalalabad 2006

Waiting to fly home Kabul 2008

With the transporter Rafi and guard Kabul 2008

Fight Night, Stillorgan Park Hotel 2010

November 2008. My Dad, Sister and Brother

The Volcanic Island of Rabaul 2011

With Matt Geyer and Scott Hill after the game

With Shane Amian and other members of the Wanderers team Port Moresby 2011

Soloman Islands 2011

Chapter 33

LEGEND FOR ONE DAY!

Rugby league is the major sport on PNG, but there is some rugby union if you look hard enough. I started playing union with a team called Wanderers, one of the more established teams in Port Moresby. I was 46 years of age. There was an Australian and myself, the rest were Papuans. I had trained with them two or three times when they informed me of a game the following weekend against Harlequins, another local team. They asked if I would like to come and play. I said I would, but only as a sub, that if they needed me they could put me on.

The game was in the main stadium; I turned up on the Saturday and togged out. For about twenty minutes I was sitting happily on the subs bench when the coach told me I was going on. So on I went, everyone on the pitch was naturally Papuan, all Pacific Islanders. I came on at a line out, took my position at the back, and of course the ball came straight to me. I caught it and all I heard was a growl and then felt a three person strong thumping as they hammered me to the ground. All fair and proper but it was still some battering. The novelty for them was the white guy with the ball. Every time I got the ball I was the main target.

Later I went to the local nightclub, Lamana. It was a very busy place, the top floor was supposedly the VIP section where whites usually went, the bottom floor was were the Papuans tended to congregate. We were downstairs because I'd played with the team and they were treating me as if I was one of their brothers and it was better craic. Straight away both the opposition and my own team gave me their respect. Out of the blue, this aggressive Papuan stepped forward and asked me,

"Hey what are you doing down here, you should be upstairs with the rest of your white trash." Although looking back the language may have been a touch more forthright.

One of our props, Shane Amean, who played for the national team, came over and said,

"You got a problem Alan?"

"No I don't think so." I shrugged.

"No there is no problem." My questioner hurriedly answered after taking one look at the hulking Shane.

Shane looked at the man and clearly said, "That is good, because he is one of our brothers."

That evening I met Bani, the classic Pacific Island beauty. She'd represented PNG in a beauty pageant years before. Bani was incomparably beautiful, like something you would imagine in your dreams from Mutiny on the Bounty. She had long dark Pacific Island hair which made her look very alluring.

"Hey you're that crazy white guy from the match earlier?"

"Yeah"

"You looked like a white spot on a domino."

I laughed. She laughed.

We got talking. She was divorced with two children, she worked and supported her family. Her husband had run off with a younger woman. We started dating, which mostly consisted of her coming round to mine for dinner, to watch some TV and going out for drives. Bani never wanted me to go to her village as she was very protective of me. She believed her family would latch on to me and would ask for money. Her view was that it was our time together and that more than anything she needed an escape from her village life. I understood very well the need for escape. The two of us were under no illusions about a joint future. She was never going to leave her country and I was never going to settle in PNG, but we did have a lovely spark and I enjoyed my time with her. We created an island of serenity and enjoyed our time together as much as we could. She was a wonderful companion and a great friend.

I was always asking her out to dinner and she kept refusing me. I could never grasp why this was. One night I asked her.

"What's the issue? Are you embarrassed to be seen with me?"

"No no, don't be silly. You will laugh if I tell you."

She eventually told me that she'd only used a knife and fork once or twice, years before visiting Australia, but never since. Made no odds to me, we ended up going out plenty.

Rugby became a big part of my life over there. It was always played at a very fast pace, owing as much to league as to union. The only downside was we always played on a dust bowl, the ground was so hard, after playing you would be cut to ribbons. I'd come back after a game and I wouldn't be able to move at all. But I was back laughing through the pain.

A few months into my stay, I had become very good friends with one of my handset and sim suppliers Jim Qui, a very successful Malaysian businessman. Jim knew I was into my rugby. While I was over in the Solomon Islands working, he phoned to tell me he had a surprise for me. The following Saturday, 25th November 2011, I was to play for the New South Wales Legends against the Queensland Legends in the National Stadium in a Rugby League State of Origin Legends Game.

At a charity auction Jim had bid and bought the guest spot on the Legends team as a gift. A guest spot in the match with the former pros: David Peachey, Australian international fullback; Nathan Blacklock, Australian international winger; Melbourne Storm winger Matt Geyer; 2000 Rugby League World Cup Champion Scott Hill; Australian International legend Cliff Lyons; Papua New Guinea International Winger and Legend Marcus Bai and former Papua New Guinea captain John Wilshire. And Alan Barry, some Irish guy who'd just taken up rugby union and had never ever played rugby league??

Despite my trepidation bordering on complete terror, I could not say no. A week or two later I found myself in a dressing room with rugby league players who'd been amongst the best the world had ever seen. I confessed to them that I'd never played rugby league, only union. They explained they didn't know much about union, but that since it was only an exhibition they reckoned I would be fine. The only thing they did tell me was that when I got tackled not to lie on the ground, but to get up and place the ball behind me. I somewhat naively said,

"Oh just like touch rugby but with contact?"

"Don't worry mate, it's an exhibition match, it won't be tough. No worries"

I should have been really worried but by then I was too excited.

The staff got wind I'd be playing and after they'd stopped laughing they promised to attend the match. At the time I was not exactly sure why they were laughing quite so much, but then they knew a lot more about rugby league than I did. I got the joke very quickly once the game began. As soon as I was tackled in fact.

I started and straight away the ball came to me. I ran with the ball and was tackled by two Queensland Legends and completely smashed. I remember thinking I was going to die, and laughing slightly crazed. I got up because I am a glutton for punishment. As the match progressed and I got hit more and more, although still less than everyone else, I realised I was enjoying myself, broken back, lost crown and all. I kicked two conversions but I didn't score a try. The match was televised on National TV and the commentator remarked as the camera zoomed in on the unknown pasty white guest player,

"I don't know who this Number 17 Alan Barry is, the guest player, but he's certainly taken a lot of punishment out there on the field today."

As the whistle blew for the end and the crowd streamed on to try to speak to their heroes, a boy ran up to me and asked me for my boots. I explained to him I was a nobody, but he was having none of it "you kicked two conversions" was his argument, I gave him my boots. I hobbled off in that strange beautiful pain sport sometimes brings. The night out after with the team was a life memory for me. I was back in Lamana nightclub with my temporary teammates after the game, when an Australian woman came up to me,

"I watched you play today. You're a league player alright, you had a great game. You must have played in England."

I smiled and nodded. "Yeah I played for Warrington." A complete lie, but I couldn't help myself.

"What's your name?"

"Adrian Bogan. I am known as the Broganator." A friend I'd played union with back in Dublin. She assured me she would look me up when she got back to Australia. A great day.

It turned out I'd lost a cap off a tooth, and I had a massive bruise the size of a tennis ball on my back for about two years afterwards. There was a lot of scar tissue damage. It wasn't until I went to Iraq that I managed to cure that injury with a really good sports massage. Luckily the game had been casual, a relatively tame version of the real thing, which has far more blood and thunder. They were some of the soundest lads I've ever met. Total characters, made me feel like one of the team. One of them had been an Australian Gladiator after he'd retired from League: Mark McGaw. I really was in the presence of true greatness.

I was back involved in life and PNG helped me get there.

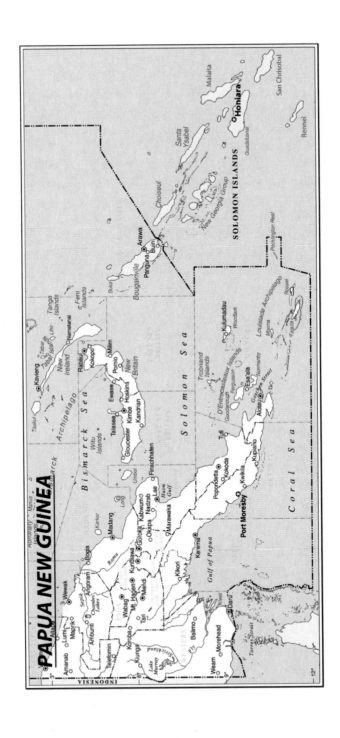

Chapter 34

BITTEN BY THE SOLOMON ISLANDS

The Solomon Islands are a truly wondrous place. The people there are very different to the Papuans. They are mostly of Melanesian descent, which means they are far more laid back and easier to get along with. When you travel out to some of the remote islands, islands such as Gizo, you are in some of the most stunningly beautiful areas in the world. There is also Kennedy Island, where a young John F Kennedy was marooned for a couple of weeks during the Second World War. JFK's PT boat had been sunk by the Japanese and he and his crew faced an arduous three and a half mile swim to what at the time was known as Plum Island.

You would often clearly see planes at the bottom of the sea, all from the Second World War, perhaps a fighter bomber still visible deep down through the crystal clear water. There were many war relics on the islands, due to the number of battles between the Americans and the Japanese during the Pacific Campaign.

On the Solomon Islands, the greatest challenge for us as a business was that the company was owned by Bemobile. Amazingly and very dishearteningly, the way the business had been set up in the Solomon Islands was even more cretinous than in PNG. It was a very small market, there were only five hundred and fifty thousand people all told on the Solomon Islands. We were competing against an organisation that was in essence Cable and Wireless (Solomon Island Telecom), so there was no paddy wackery.

The Japanese had built a large airbase outside of Guadalcanal during the war. Some 70 years later while we were building our new mobile tower there, we found an old Second World War 1000lb bunker buster bomb. The authorities were called and we waited for the army to show up. Nope, two local police turned up and put it on the back of their truck using a winch and trundled off in their flatbed truck, bomb bouncing all the way. I guess it's difficult to worry about health and safety if your island is broke. Divers would pay a lot of money to dive off the islands, in and amongst the perfect, unspoilt reefs, the tropical fish and the sunken wrecks. Tourism was everything on the islands.

The flight between Port Moresby and Honiara was five hours. The only way to get around the islands themselves was by boat or light aircraft. I had a team there full time, a member of which was an alcoholic Irishman, Seamus. He used to turn up every morning for work reeking of booze. The only good news for him was that he never got malaria. I presume the mosquitos knew better than to bite him, for they'd surely have dropped dead. Seamus was another one of the feckless diaspora I have found all over the world – guys and girls squirreled away doing an awful job, but getting paid and enjoying their privilege. Seamus was the sales manager, an idiot and a raving piss artist.

The first time we worked together was a Friday up in Gizo, we decided we'd go out for a couple of drinks. We got absolutely hammered, smashed, you name it. Next day I woke up, a tomahawk hangover through my head. We both just about made it to the plane. I slept the whole way back to Honiara while Seamus drank. In Honiara he was in the accommodation beside me. I was due to fly back to Port Moresby on the Sunday morning. I was sitting out the back, facing the sea with my laptop out, doing a bit of work. As I'm listening to the sea, Seamus strolls past me with a can of beer.

"You fancy going out for a drink?"

I laughed, "Are you for real we only stopped drinking at four o clock this morning"

He was serious. "Yeah but it's the weekend." Him and his big red nose. Very few people have ever got under my skin like Seamus. I can't explain it and I am not going to attempt to, it is just one of those things. I must say he was not a bad guy and to be fair he did try his best. However, the more he tried the more irritating I found him.

When we launched 3G on the Solomon Islands, I got the worst case of malaria possible, short of dying. It was the 3rd December 2011. We'd invited the government to the launch. The deputy Prime Minister got so drunk he fell into the pool and the leader of the opposition, who was also the ex-Prime Minister, got so drunk he started abusing myself and the company secretary. The company secretary was an English man who we'd dubbed Little Britain for his resemblance to the bald headed guy on the Little Britain TV show. The leader of the opposition informed us we were white trash and were treating the Islanders like servants. In other words a truly epic night. The free bar ran from seven o clock until eternity. Pacific Islanders love to drink, so it was a match made in heaven.

I went home to bed sober as I had been working. I woke up the next day without the mosquito net and the window open, my feet were covered in bites. I should have noticed the open window going to bed but I didn't. I went back to PNG and felt fine for about two weeks. I'd almost forgotten about it. The 16th of December rolled around, the company Christmas party. I was due to fly home on the 21st. I'd arranged two days before that in Singapore for meetings with suppliers. The afternoon of the 16th, I mentioned to Little Britain that I had a very sore throat and a headache. He didn't hesitate.

"Malaria mate, I've had it twice. It's definitely malaria. Go and get yourself a testing kit."

I did and the self-testing kit came up negative. Being a malarial idiot, I naturally thought I was away with it. I went ahead and hosted the Christmas party for the staff. I felt wretched all night and I only drank tonic. I went home early enough, woke up a couple of hours later, drenched in sweat from head to foot, like I'd had a shower. I rang a friend.

"I need a doctor."

"Mate, they're not going to send a doctor out to you. You have to go and see them in a clinic."

"I cannot get out of this bed."

I have a very high pain threshold but this completely annihilated me. The doctor was eventually convinced to come and see me. She told me that on a scale of one to ten, I was ten for malaria. I had won the top prize for malaria, no mean feat on the Solomon's. The disease had incubated in my body over the two weeks since the bites. She gave me two shots and a course of anti-malaria tablets. For two days I felt like death warmed up. I still went to work though, I had too much to do and I was really conscious of wanting to get back to Ireland in time for Christmas. At least I had that Sunday free to spend all day in bed; on the Monday I went to our weekly management meeting. I wasn't hallucinating, but besides that tiny mercy I'd every other thing wrong with me that you could imagine. Horrific. The tablets helped at least.

By the time the 21st rolled around, I was well enough to get on the flight to Singapore. Our handset supplier there had planned a big Christmas party for me in what are called KTV bars in Singapore. KTV bars are karaoke bars with strippers. The last thing on earth I wanted or needed at that time was a KTV bar. I was booked into the Marina Bay Sands hotel, a really beautiful hotel overlooking the Singapore Bay. All I wanted was to relax in my room in preparation for my flight home to Ireland and spending my Christmas with my children; but I was the one being feted and even though I still had no interest in the KTV bars, I hadn't really got much of a choice as my supplier insisted I attend. I staggered through two days of meetings and celebrations. I was feeling rough after the malaria, probably more drained than anything. There was one upside though, I'd lost a lot of weight.

For Christmas in Dublin I'd decided to treat myself, so I'd booked into the Shelbourne Hotel on St Stephen's Green. I arrived home Christmas Eve 2011. It was an incredible feeling. I'd never come home so close to Christmas before. Christmas Eve is the perfect day to arrive into Dublin: truly a wonderful winter experience. I checked into the Shelbourne, into a beautiful historic room. Then I went and met my children. We all had dinner; afterwards walking down Grafton Street, nearly freezing to death creating memories I will have forever – a truly memorable day after been away from my family for the previous number of months. That evening before I went out, I heard a knock while lying on the bed in the Shelbourne. It was the staff coming around with a hamper, a real treat. That evening I went out with my friends, and although I was pretty much off the drink and food I still thoroughly enjoyed myself. I spent Christmas morning with my children. My family were happy and so was I.

I'd left Ireland and a lot of trauma behind me at the beginning of that year. I was back healed.

I was back to me.

Chapter 35

A FAMILY MAN ABROAD

There was much fun to be had in PNG, but there was also the serious side to the job and that was being up against Digicel. Our main competitor was involved in all manner of cunning activities and we had to be equally as sharp. I was enjoying myself again.

Our own network was falling apart. This was being exacerbated by a major shareholder dispute between Hong Kong Investment Company, who were milking the business dry and the government, the IPBC, who felt they were not getting anything out of it. The government could not get rid of HKIC because they were contractually bound to them but what they could do was make life difficult for them. We were all working under this completely dysfunctional board that had run out of funding.

I was blessed with an amazing team, who I'd moulded and who in turn did me proud. They'd seen all the expats come and go and they knew I was there to win, similar to how I used to work in Afghanistan. My marketing manager Judith, a Papuan, was excellent and I learnt a lot from her and, I would hope, her from me. Between Judith and my graphic designer Rasheed we came up with some great campaigns. We worked on focusing on our strengths, which were few and far between.

I had been in PNG for about a year when Andy came out of a board meeting and told me he'd been asked to resign. HKIC was not happy with Andy and got rid of him much to my disgust. Andy was a victim of boardroom politics, plain and simple. It was a crazy decision. HKIC had convinced the government to let them try one more person. I was introduced to this person from Hong Kong, who I can only describe as a complete and utter clown: a former accountant with no experience of the industry who knew nothing. He was an American who'd been living in Hong Kong. In reality he was living in a dream world – another puppet for the Hong Kong circus troop.

I tried to work with the new American CEO for around two months. By then my contract was up for renewal. Coincidentally, at this same time I received a call from Violet. It was a Saturday morning and I was still in bed. I knew it was serious when I saw her name. It had just gone 7pm back in Ireland so it was about 6am in Moresby and she was hysterical. Our youngest Connor had been hit by a car outside Wesley Youth Disco in Dublin. It wasn't clear yet the extent of his injuries. I did manage to ascertain that they were not immediately life threatening. I felt helpless. I spent an hour anxiously pacing up and down until Violet rang me back. Connor had been very lucky, his only injury was a severely fractured ankle. The doctors couldn't operate because the ankle was too swollen, they needed to reset his ankle. He was in excruciating pain. Connor has the makings of a decent rugby player and a fine athlete and I really didn't want to see that disappear, but at the time I was just thankful he was OK.

I told my new boss I needed some time off to go home to see my son. He said no, even though I'd only had around four weeks off the previous year. He said I couldn't go. I figured I could handle life without the job, as I was not particularly enjoying the new working conditions. I handed in my notice, whereupon he told me I could take my holiday. But my mind was made up. Three different CEO's was two too many. All in all, it was a lesson in how to screw up a business. My son needed me back in Ireland, but more than that I needed to be there for him.

Leaving PNG and my team was painful. We'd worked hard and the bonds had grown fast and quick, we'd come through a lot together. They came to see me off at the airport and they cried because they knew nothing good was going to come of me leaving. We'd had to put up with three CEOs in a year. For the team it was worse, they'd just lost their immediate boss and I was being replaced by an Aussie blackguard, who I'd already cautioned for groping the female staff and using one of the male staff as a tea boy.

I was leaving them to the drunken wolves no doubt. I bought them presents and whereas maybe in the past I would have stayed, I felt things more deeply now and I needed to be near my son. No bones about it though, the staff were the ones who really lost. They did not have the option to walk away, and as anyone can attest to, working in a job under those types of conditions can wear you all the way down. Digicel were the real winners, as our team was destroyed.

Personally I felt like a new man. I had a career again. I had some respect. I felt like the problems were behind me. Being an adult, you simply move on to the next challenge. Luckily, and in fairness to my former employers, they paid me the bonus I was due so the hard work had paid off.

The company went into partnership with Vodafone soon after.

As well as saying goodbye to my team, another thing I had to do was to tell Bani that I was leaving PNG for good. In the time I knew her she had never once put any pressure on me in terms of our relationship or financially. We had grown very close and I truly did care for her. Saying goodbye to someone that you care about is an exceptionally difficult thing to do. It is a credit to her that when I told her about my son, the first thing she said was you need to go home. I knew she wouldn't take any money from me, so I went out and bought a new TV and left it with a colleague on the instructions that he was to call her the following day and tell her that I had left a present in the office . I just wanted her to be able to treat herself and this was no different from any man back in Ireland wanting to treat his girlfriend with a present . When the plane took off from Port Moresby, I looked down and thought to myself, I hope one I can return as a tourist and meet up with the many friends I made, and who knows maybe even Bani.

One of my favourite stories while in PNG concerned Graham Woodruff, an English accountant in Bemobile. Graham was a character straight out of a Graham Green novel. Outwardly mild mannered, he alone out of the whole office wore a full suit and tie every day. Ah the English and their uniforms. He also used a real cup and saucer for his tea. I played golf with Graham most Sundays and we would chat about the usual fluff. He was always telling me how much he loved his wife and family. He was a skinny, very slight looking individual and looked exactly like an accountant. There were a couple of things about him that did not fit, he had a temper that would flare up from time to time, and there was always the suggestion of an unrevealed side to him. I got on well with him, despite him constantly telling me how much he loved his wife and how much he loathed Andy our CEO every single time we went golfing.

One day we were all shocked and horrified to learn that poor Graham had been kidnapped. We understood the implications. We knew that meant we all were at risk. Suddenly we were confronted with what we would do if we were kidnapped, and we all missed our family that much more. The police came and interviewed everyone, asked if any of us had noticed anything out of the ordinary, being followed or any suspicious characters. None of us had, but we were still frightened.

Next the police went through Graham's phone records, one local number showed up more than all the others. It belonged to Graham's house maid. Graham had called her an hour after he'd been kidnapped. He was a great employer, he had probably called to give her the day off once he knew he'd been kidnapped.

Frankly the cops were getting suspicious at this stage and they used the signal from Graham's phone to triangulate his whereabouts – surprisingly poor job by the kidnappers not to ditch his phone. They tracked him to a house in the middle of nowhere, off the beaten track. They found Graham alone, wearing his suit, making himself a jam sandwich, no doubt thinking about how much he loved his wife. His company car was outside the house, the house which belonged to his house maid who he may or may not have been kissing.

Weirdly the police were not satisfied with Graham's descriptions of his kidnapping ordeal. They probably roughed him up a bit during the month he spent in the PNG prison. He couldn't have held out, not Graham.

Graham had had a very strained relationship with Andy the CEO and had orchestrated a kidnapping, but unfortunately for Graham, Andy had left PNG the previous week. Graham did not have the heart to have anyone else kidnapped so he did the only honourable thing, he kidnapped himself. The police eventually let him get off with a deportation and there was never another kidnapping again.

I have spoken to him since and Graham is adamant he was framed, that the kidnappers had stolen his golf clubs. Who really knows?

Chapter 36

Bored in Iraq and smiling in Uganda

I left PNG for good just in time to get back for my son's operation. The operation was being performed by one of the best orthopaedic surgeons in Ireland.

"This is bad." The surgeon did not pull any punches, he painted a very bleak picture.

Connor's ankle turned out to be fractured and dislocated. I happily ferried him around for three months as he healed. I made sure he did not do any weight bearing and that he went in to have his dressing changed on his open wound from the surgery every 48 hours. Violet had a fulltime job so it worked out well. I was able to be there to ensure everything went smoothly. It struck me that I liked being back in Ireland. I spent three months with Connor ensuring he fully recovered. In the end he returned to rugby with both his school team and our family club, DLSP.

I updated my resume to include PNG, and alongside the Afghan adventure, I was developing a name as someone who could do a job in foreign climes, an international trouble shooter. Although I was unemployed again, this time things were not critical. Sure enough, I received another contact from LinkedIn, an email written by a man called Jihad from Iraq. Sentences you never expect to read, a man called Jihad emailed me from Iraq. It read,

"Hi Alan I've just looked at your profile on LinkedIn we are looking for an acting CEO in Iraq. I was wondering whether you would be interested?" I half thought it was a sick joke. However I knew enough to know I did not know enough, so I mailed him back, giving him my mobile number in Ireland.

Jihad phoned me back ten minutes later. He was acting on behalf of Newroz Telecom, situated in Erbil, Northern Iraq, in the semi-autonomous Kurdistan. Newroz is jointly owned by Vtel holdings, my old friends from the failed Afghan Wireless deal a thousand years ago. The other owner was a Kurdish company.

"Our CEO has to go for an operation, and he has tasked me with finding someone who could come in on an interim basis, while he is incapacitated. Would you be interested?"

"Sounds really interesting. Sure I would definitely be interested"

The following day I received an email from the secretary of the Vtel board of directors in Amman, Jordan. They flew me over to Amman for a meeting. Business class return, always a good indicator of a serious offer. I met with the Vtel board. Sure enough they remembered me from Afghanistan, which is how they found me on LinkedIn. It was not a coincidence.

"We want you." Was pretty much their approach.

They were keen for me to take the job, on condition the main local shareholder, a Kurd called Kawa who wore his heart on his sleeve, gave me his blessing, which he did. I always had a lot of time for him and I enjoyed working with him. He was really direct but a first class operator, very like Amin Ramin, my old MD in AWCC.

I was temporarily replacing a man called Abu Omar. In the Islamic world, it is considered a great honour to be called Abu followed by your eldest son's name, in this case Omar. He was a straight talker, and a Palestinian: a very pleasant man to deal with, whom I saw little of except for the handover. I started the following week. It was August 2012 when I took over.

I was acting CEO and the job was OK. I was being well remunerated, but the problem I and everyone else had was that there was absolutely nothing to do outside work. That is not exactly true; there was one thing you could do there, drink. 90% of the expats there were verging on if not complete alcoholics. Watch sport on TV, drink and eat; that was our lot. I succumbed in my own way, particularly with the eating. Try as I might, becoming an alcoholic was a bridge too far for me.

Whilst many wanted to avoid the bar, we really had very little choice. I was there all winter; the temperature dropped to a freezing –20°C. Far too bloody cold to go home, you'd freeze to death, the only way to stay warm at home was using paraffin heater death traps that were lethal if left burning overnight. Unlike in Afghanistan there were no open fires. So I, like everyone else, spent most evenings congregated in a bar or a restaurant. Everybody drank every single day, then drove home, getting into cars when they could barely stand up. I began to fall into drinking pretty heavily as well.

I lived in the Christian quarter of Erbil, in a place called Ankawa. All of the bars and restaurants were in Ankawa, as the Christians were allowed to sell alcohol. The Muslims had to come to Ankawa if they wanted a drink. The street I lived on there were mostly Iraqi Christians who had fled Baghdad to get away from the ethnic cleansing. Fascinating people. There was a Christian church on my street. I wanted to see a Christian service. One of the staff, a Kurdish Christian, took me there. They were Assyrian, Catholics who talk in the tongue of Christ, Aramaic, and are amongst the original peoples of what is now Iraq. Visiting their Chaldean Catholic church was a very spiritual experience for me.

Besides the Assyrians, Northern Iraq and Erbil is the home of the Peshmerga and the Kurds. Saladin the greatest hero of the Arab world, the most revered of all Arabic kings, was a Kurd interestingly enough – a fact very few people are aware of and certainly something I didn't know until my arrival in Erbil. Saladin was the leader of the Arab Army that captured Jerusalem in 1187 from the Crusaders. In Kurdistan Islam is mostly the Shafi'i school of Sunni Islam, one of the four schools of Sunni Islam in Islamic Law.

There were the Yazidis, ancient Christians who worship the angels and were once a considerable minority in the region. The Yazidis are regarded as devil worshippers by ISIS, the news media moniker for the so called Islamic State, and have been targeted by the group in order to cleanse Iraq of non-Muslims. Once upon a time there were also a lot of Jews in Iraq, until Saddam drove them all out. Nowadays what is left of that region's once diverse religious population is involved in a fight to the death with ISIS. The various religions are scattered. The heroic and fearsome Kurdish Peshmerga are seemingly doing most of the fighting against the forces of darkness ISIS represents.

I could have partaken more in the local carousing, but I was acting GM-CEO meaning I could not let myself go too much. Besides which, did my colleagues really want to hang around with their boss? I tended to watch a lot of TV.

Erbil was safe, probably safer than Port Moresby, but outside the city, it was a different story. ISIS had not yet reared their hydra head but Syria was fully flowing, engulfed by civil war. There were a lot of refugees in and around the city. The nightly decision to drink and eat or eat and drink was wearing me down for sure. There were no golf courses, there was the odd football pitch, and we used to play five a side in between the bouts of boozy boredom.

When it snowed, you'd wake up in the morning and breathe and the room would mist up like you'd been sleeping in a bed in the Phoenix Park all night. I couldn't leave the paraffin heater on because the fumes would kill me. My social life was a solitary chair I had placed in front of the TV and a blanket.

In the summer time it was roasting. We could go and drink outside in the German beer garden, listen to some lovely music. Then the next day you could get up, go shopping, go for a coffee, watch TV and go drink outside in the German beer garden. I didn't notice it as much in Afghanistan, as I was in a house with four others and I was not acting CEO, hence I could partake more in the nightly festivities.

Nine months of good money and boredom. Thankfully once every two months I had to go to board meetings in Amman. Those bimonthly meetings in Amman became something to look forward to, somewhat manic and angry but at least they were a change. Typically I would be there for a few days. In the meetings everyone would spend their time giving out about each other, beginning the discussions in English and then continuing on into Arabic so I couldn't understand, or more likely so they could give full vent to their expletives about whomever. Eventually I reported the figures and they would ask me various vexed questions.

On one of the trips to Amman, I was asked to remain for a further meeting the following week. This gave me a weekend to spend in Amman all to myself. Being away from Erbil was a welcome break and an opportunity to visit some of the sites in the Holy Land. This was a truly spiritual experience and something I would highly recommend. Whether you are religious or not, it's something worth seeing: a soul cleansing exercise that we could all do with. I visited the exact location that John the Baptist baptised Jesus. It was a very spiritual place, where I could sense a strange kind of peace and tranquillity, a feeling of ease and calmness that was most welcome.

I visited mount Nebo where, according to Christian tradition, Moses was buried, although his burial site is not specified. There is also a Byzantine church and monastery, which house the famous Byzantine mosaics. Again this part of the day filled me with thousands of years of history and a great feeling of serenity that was good for the soul. The final part of the day was a trip to Madaba and the Church of St George. Constructed in AD560, it is filled with mosaics of St George and the Dragon. The ancient presence of the Crusaders who battled for the Holy Land thousands of years ago was everywhere. It was a very enjoyable weekend and I feel blessed to have been given the opportunity to visit those amazing locations. This is one of the advantages of the expat experience.

The Palestinian CEO Abu Omar had gone to the States for his operation and then returned to Palestine to recuperate. When he was well enough to return to Erbil, the Israelis would not let him out of Palestine because he had so many Iraqi visas on his passport. That meant another three months on top of the contract for me. Nonetheless, it was a happy day when I left. The only thing to report from Iraq at that time was that there was nothing to report. Hard to reconcile that dull place with the hell hole it has become of late at the hands of ISIS.

I was at home in Ireland after I finished up with my Iraqi adventure when I received a call from an old friend telling me he'd recommended me for a job in Uganda. About half an hour later an email came through from a company called

Smile Communications. Smile had won a 4G LTE licence in Uganda. LTE is another phrase for 4G; it stands for long-term evolution, and is high speed connectivity on the internet. They had launched in June and this was now early July. The launch could have gone better and they needed help.

I got the phone call from HR telling me she had heard great things about me. They wanted me to come in as head of sales and marketing, but as a consultant. It was a step down but the salary was the same grade as a CEO. I agreed terms on a 6 month contract, got on a plane and flew out to Uganda.

What I arrived into was difficult to handle at first. They'd launched the new network with all of the retail outlets in the wrong place, with no footfall and no potential customers. They were even in the wrong socio-economic areas. 4G was a high end product and Smile had opened outlets in low income areas where people had little or no interest, and definitely no surplus income. The average monthly spend on the product was $100; the outlets were in areas where average wage was $100 a month. The planning had been poor, hence my predecessor being asked to fall on his sword. The search was on for a new sales and marketing director of African origin, as that was company policy.

The marketing campaign was a triumph in obscurity, nobody understood what Smile LTE 4G did. The marketing manager before me had paid an advertising agency too many dollars to come up with a billboard campaign that was confusing and nobody was able to understand. When you looked at the billboard, you couldn't make out what the overall message was. So again we needed to fix the message.

Firstly, I simplified the marketing message, so that people could understand what we did. I brought it back to basics. I had to work with the sales team to motivate them as well as closing down, repositioning and reopening retail points in the right areas.

Before I'd arrived, they'd fired half the sales team. Morale was as hard to find as the sales outlets or the marketing message. I worked with those people for a month.

For the rest of my professional career, I will always regard what I achieved in six months in Uganda as something special. Although it was only six months, I am exceptionally proud of what we achieved. Thrown in as a consultant, not an iota of support, never any recognition for what my team achieved and how we turned things around. They portrayed me as the big bad consultant sent in from head office, but in reality I was very popular with the locals. I'd been sent there to clean up management's mess. Hence management were not overly fond of me. At my very first meeting with the sales team, I gave them my usual introductory sales speech:

"I'm here to help you, I am here to work with you, I am here to help each and every one of you to succeed. But the only way that I can help you succeed is if you help yourself.

You will find me very fair. You will find me a person who can be approached, if I can coach or mentor you I will. I will help you all to be successful."

I finished with,

"I want you all to watch a famous clip of Alec Baldwin in a movie called *Glengarry Glen Ross*."

When I give my pep talk I like to quote the Alec Baldwin speech from the film based on the play by David Mamet. I played the clip on Youtube[29] of the iconic speech when he tells Jack Lemmon's character that he can't have coffee because coffee is for closers. Or the other one when Alec Baldwin puts his watch down on the desk in front of Ed Harris and says,

"See that watch, it costs more than your car."

They are both exceptionally motivational speeches and a great way to subtly get a very valuable message across, while at the same time having some fun. Fun, something that was needed to lift the doom and gloom hanging over the Ugandan sales team. The team were so into it that *Glengarry Glen Ross* became the theme of our weekly sales meeting. I'd find out who beat their target for that week and on the way to the office

---

29 https://www.youtube.com/watch?v=v9XW6P0tiVc

Friday morning I'd pick up whatever number of coffees I needed. The first meeting I bought coffee only for myself.

"I'm buying coffee for myself because I'm a closer, I wish I was sharing it with you," would be my opening speech every week to the sales team at our 8am meeting.

Then I had to buy two coffees, then three. I had 23 sales team members in direct sales. By the time I left I was getting everyone a coffee on the way to the Friday morning sales meeting. We'd generated a wonderful team spirit. I left a very successful sales team and a business that was increasing its revenues every month. I also handed back a highly successful marketing and commercial department, with a clearly defined marketing message. All achieved in a country I'd not known a single thing about until I landed at the start of the six months: a highly, highly enjoyable experience.

Ugandans are incredible people: very easy to get along with; slightly shy and reserved; really good to work with. Presumably a lot of their reserved nature is a learnt trait from the terrifying time of Amin. They had 15 presidents between Idi Amin and the current president Yoweri Museveni. Museveni has been in power since 1986 and although not everyone likes him he seems to have returned some measure of stability to the country. There are no civil wars and it is safe. I think if I hadn't had my children back in Ireland I might have stayed on. Kampala was a great place. From day one taking on the role full time was never on the cards. I was doing the job of head of sales and marketing, but getting the salary of a CEO. To be honest the GM was a very nice lady, but she was out of her depth. I find it difficult to suffer fools gladly. I tried my best to just ignore her.

Obviously I'd long come to realise that expats are not all great. I've come across people and I have thought to myself, how the hell did they get this job? And normally it was the old story, they just kept their head down and played politics better than they could do the job itself. A qualification that I don't have.

I have also come across some really excellent colleagues, expat or otherwise. I don't want to give the impression that I am the only person who can do the job. Politics is an important part of life and sadly it's never been my strong point. I have always tried to let my results and delivery do the talking.

The one thing that I have always prided myself on was the standard of the work that I do. When the staff found out I was leaving, they sent 38 emails asking for me to be kept on. But it was not to be and I walked away with my head held high and no regrets. Contract work can be thankless at times but that is the way of it.

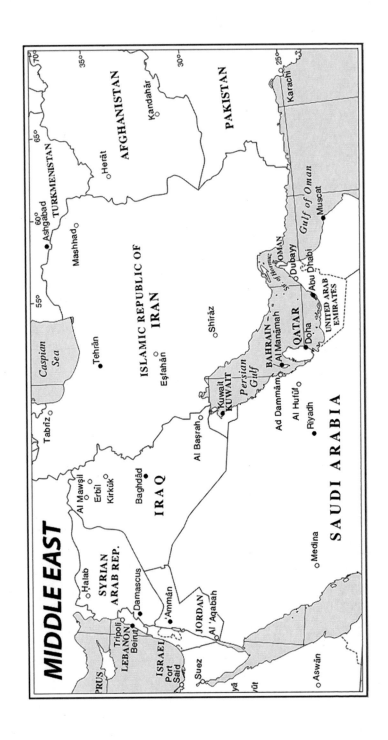

Chapter 37

Both sides

Twenty years ago I could not have lived openly in Ireland. Even now it's still at the back of my mind, writing this book and talking about some of my military experiences has posed some challenges. The army drummed it into us: keep a working cover story at all times. I have blown my cover story out the door in writing this book. Up until now, I had always shied away from talking about my past with any candour.

After I returned to Ireland in the late nineties, Violet came home one day and there was a car with two occupants in the driveway. She pulled in and they pulled off. She phoned me straight away, the burglaries in the UK were at the back of her mind. I phoned the local Garda station. After a couple of pleasantries,

"Oh an English accent, are you ex-military by chance?"

"Yes I am actually."

"Could you hold the line please?" A Special Branch detective came on and asked me,

"Where do you live? What time are you home at?" We arranged to meet.

Right enough he called up that evening. Violet and I stood in front of him after shaking hands and he looked at me and asked,

"Why didn't you tell us you were living here?" This was 1998. He continued,

"Do you realise there are two active service units in this area alone? One of them down the road?" It had never occurred to me. For me after the signing of the Good Friday Agreement the war was over.

The detective was not exaggerating. A few weeks later, the Real IRA tried to hold up a Securicor van in Ashford, Wicklow. Six members of a Real IRA active service unit were involved in trying to hijack the van, five were caught and imprisoned and one was shot dead. The Guards had ambushed them. So there I was, a guy who had served on all manner of operations, living pretty much down the road from two active service units. The detective was right, I should have mentioned it.

Even more incredulously, not long after the first attempted hijacking I was happily commuting back and forth to the UK. My English colleagues and friends would ask,

"Are you not worried living in Ireland, you know the IRA, bombs and the Troubles?"

I used to just laugh at them; for me Dublin was idyllic and peaceful. Nobody ever seemed overly concerned with what religion you were – a million miles from the North despite it being an hour away in the car. I was in my office one Tuesday in 1999, ignoring the TV screen on the wall. A colleague asked me as I was busying myself with paperwork,

"Where was it you said you lived again?" I was getting a bit fed up with the questions.

"Dalkey," I answered.

"Dall key?" she repeated pronouncing the silent 'L',

"Yeah" I answered a little irked.

"It's on Sky News."

I wasn't really in the humour, but I looked up and sure enough there on Sky News was a picture of Dalkey Village. I turned up the volume to listen to the report of a raid on a Brinks Allied van on Sorrento Road in Dalkey, home to some of the wealthiest people in Ireland. The Continuity IRA this time, used two vans, one fitted with an iron girder, to ram a Brink Allied cash in transit van. The gang rammed the van with the girder, giving them access to the money while the van's security guards were held at gunpoint.

Once they loaded all their loot, the gunmen armed with AK47s sped off in a Ford Granada they'd bought. Unfortunately for them, it broke down one mile away at the Dalkey Island Hotel. The raiders proceeded to hijack another car, a passing red Saab. They ordered the couple out of the car and then fired a shot, which grazed the driver, he was not seriously injured. The gang took off in the Red Saab along Coliemore Road, leaving behind most of their loot.

Neil was a British friend who lived in Dalkey around that time. Neil had been out walking his dog down Coliemore road minding his own business. He stopped to watch as the gang's Granada sped down the road, and as they piled out of it after the break down. He stood there enthralled as they waved down the red Saab and ushered the man and his partner out onto the road, firing a shot in the air that seemed to catch the innocent driver. Neil saw the gang get into the red Saab and speed off. He couldn't believe his luck getting to watch a film shoot up close, especially one that looked so realistic. He didn't find out until afterwards that he and his shih tszu Basil were witnessing a real carjacking and a robbery getaway. He'd wanted to applaud.

Of course my British colleagues watched the story unfolding alongside me, looking at me, shaking their heads,

"You must be mad living over there. It looks like chaos."

They didn't really understand how out of place this all was in Brigadoon.

Standing in my office in the UK listening to all my colleagues' advice from crime free Britain, I remember being worried that Violet would get stuck in the resulting traffic driving the kids home.

Ireland is home and home is safe, right?

I live in Ireland and it's my home, I love this country, however quite often I get comments from people I know about my past and the job I did. They see the role I performed in the North as some form of betrayal.

I don't.

I was a young man who actually discovered his own national identity as a result of being exposed to that sectarian drivel, and I am proud of the job I did.

I have never met anyone who would describe themselves as pro IRA, but the issue I constantly have thrown in my face when people discover I served in the British Army is,

"But you're Irish, how could you have done it?"

When I explain that I am also a passionate royalist and monarchist they come again at me,

"How can you be like that? You're Irish." And I feel like screaming, just like I did at that RUC officer all those years ago, "Yeah I am, so what?"

If you look at the Royal Standard there is an Irish harp. That symbol represents the many Irish who love this country and would be happy if Ireland was still part of the Commonwealth. I personally think we wouldn't have had half the problems we have seen over the past 92 years if DeValera hadn't got such a grip back after independence in 1922.

I have more respect for men who took up arms for what they believed in than an idiot who proclaims his politics from an armchair or a bar stool. There is one acquaintance I know in particular, every time we meet he slips in remarks about the Brits and jibes about England. At first it was funny, but after 7 years of listening to him it's quite clear that he, like many others, has a real hang-up about the English. To my mind this individual is nothing more than a chocolate Republican, an armchair Provo. There are others, they harp and harp on about it. The funny thing is they have no idea. They've no idea what it was like, any of it: the North, being a soldier in the Forgotten War. I'm not sure I understand it myself, how could they?

Chapter 38

FINALE

I'm pretty sure that is the end of the story. I am back to the old me or maybe it is the new me. My head is on straight and back to normal. I look forward to the future.

How do I describe my story? I was a chancer of sorts, I was someone who got through life and everything I touched turned to gold. I believed I could sell sand to Arabs and snow to Eskimos, but I learned I could never sell blarney to the Irish. I started to believe my own sales pitch, and that's when I started having problems. I was a great salesman, but like any good salesman when you start believing your own pitch you fool yourself. Why? I lost the run of myself because no matter what obstacle I was faced with, whether that be in the military on the verge of being shot, being in Afghanistan, whatever I did in life I'd always come up smelling of roses.

2010 that all stopped. 2010, the year it all started falling apart. Everything happened at once. I lost that ability to think on my feet; I lost my fighting spirit; I lost the ability to cut a deal, to hustle, to make things happen. I became a loser, and I remember being a loser for approximately twelve months. And instead of feeling positive about life, I started to feel sorry for myself. I started to think woe is me, instead of thinking of how to get myself out of my situation. The only positive I can bring out of that awful chapter, was that I came out of it a much better person. When I went into it I was a cocky arrogant jerk, when I came out of it I was humble. I now understand and believe that everyone deserves a chance, that there is an innate goodness inside everyone, even the ghouls who tried so hard to bring me low. I will never be judgemental of anyone ever again. That is my promise to myself.

I got married because it was the right thing to do. I grew to love my wife because she became my companion and my best friend. When the marriage eventually broke down in 2008, I still loved her . It was the reverse of the way it should have been.

The fact that our marriage broke up when it did was one of the reasons I found life so difficult. All of a sudden, after 22 years, I was on my own. Normally people when they split up have grown apart, for me I had grown towards her. But on reflection we had nothing left really, perhaps only an old friendship and a marriage that had zero trust both ways and absolutely no respect. I have never felt a stronger love for anyone than when she gave birth to all three of our children. For that alone I feel blessed.

Sure Violet and I have had our ups and downs – in the later years, lots of downs and very few ups – but when I look back on my life in general, I can safely say there are only three or four of those fifty years I regret. The opportunity to live and work all over the world; the people I have met who have helped and influenced me; the people I have hopefully influenced in their lives; the difference I have been able to make in distant countries; the chance to be successful; the love I have received from my family, the choices I have been able to give them in life.

On one of my final nights in the Solomon Islands as a celebration with the team, we hired a boat and went out to a lazy little perfect island. We marooned ourselves away from our lives for just one night. The island was surreal and beautiful. The delicious sweet warm air allowing us to smile and play moonlit drunken castaways. It was an uproarious bender. For some reason, everyone felt safe and let go. Sometimes you just catch the wave in this life, that night we caught it plum. Coming back to the main island through the inky black night, sea like a mirror, cigarettes bouncing around us like fireflies, the exaltation at being alive in the midst of paradise. I could see the Milky Way and all the constellations up close, the most amazing sky I had ever witnessed in my life. A year before I had been on Killiney Hill looking up at that same moon and sky.

I'll always remember that boat ride as when I finally came down off that hill.

Bibliography

Black, B., 2010. 'Kabul Bank: Where They Don't Fear The Regulators Enough To Even Hide The Abuses.' *Business Insider(US)*, 7 September .

Carl, A. & Garasu, L., 2002. 'Weaving consensus: The Papua New Guinea – Bougainville peace process.' *Accord,* Issue 12.

Ellis, E., 2004. 'Wireless Wars.' *Fortune International (Europe)*, 18 October, 150(7), p. 68.

Ellis, E., 2010. 'Why Farnood was Flushed Out of Kabul Bank.' *Euromoney*, 1 November.

Filkins, D., 2011. 'The Afghan Bank Heist.' *The New Yorker*, 14 February.

Freeman, M. F. & Kator-Mubarez , A., 2014. *KIRK MEYER, FORMER DIRECTOR OF THE AFGHAN THREAT FINANCE CELL.*
[Online]
Available at: https://globalecco.org/
kirk-meyer-former-director-of-the-afghan-threat-finance-cell
[Accessed 29 April 2015].

Hastings, P., 2011. *Telephone Systems International and Ehsanollah Bayat Defeat US$400 Million Claim Brought by Lord Michael Cecil, Stuart Bentham and Alexander Grinling Bringing 9 Years of Litigation to a Close,* London: PR Newswire.

Kyle, T., 2013. 'Incredible Story of the British soldier who was the only survivor of a 19th century conquest – and the warnings for today's military missions.' *The Daily Mail*, 25 March.

Masterova, A., Partlow, J. & Higgins, A., 2010. 'In Afghanistan, signs of crony capitalism.' *Washington Post*, 22 February.

Morauta, T. R. H. M., 2011. *The theft and waste of public money in Papua New Guinea's Public Enterprises*, Port Moresby: The Ministry for Public Enterprises.

Quentin Sommerville, BBC, 2013. *Kabul Bank fraud: Sherkhan Farnood and Khalilullah Ferozi jailed.* [Online] Available at: http://www.bbc.com/news/world-asia-21666689 [Accessed 9 March 2015].

Rose, D., 2011. 9/11 'The Tapping Point.' *Vanity Fair*, September.

Rose, D., 2012. 'Robbed and Ruined by a British Court on the orders of the CIA...And we couldn't tell a soul: The chilling story of how secret justice cost a couple their £5m home – and £700m business.' *Mail on Sunday*, 8 April.

Wells, M., 2001. 'How smart was this bomb?' *The Guardian*, 19 November.